EYEWITNESS
OCEAN

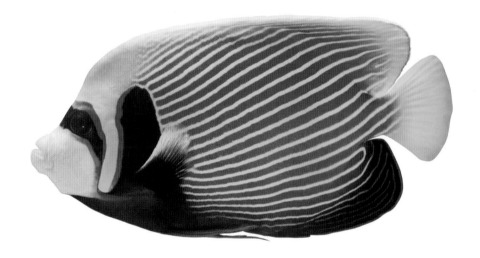

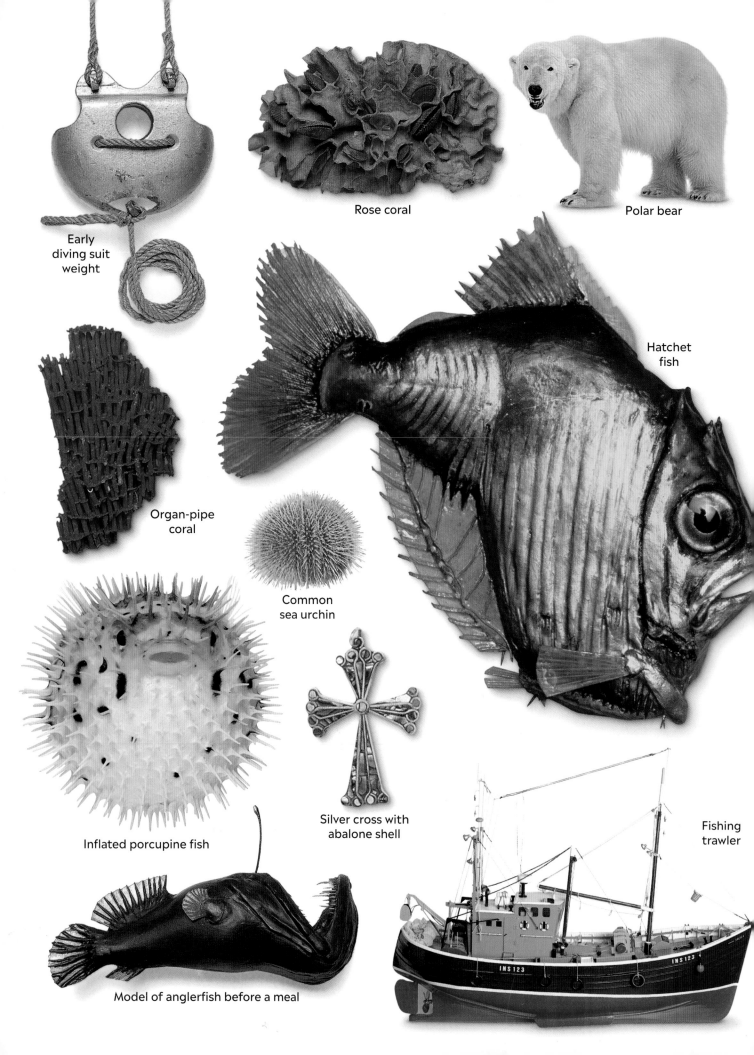

Early
diving suit
weight

Rose coral

Polar bear

Organ-pipe
coral

Common
sea urchin

Hatchet
fish

Inflated porcupine fish

Silver cross with
abalone shell

Fishing
trawler

Model of anglerfish before a meal

EYEWITNESS

OCEAN

AUTHOR **DR. MIRANDA MACQUITTY**
PHOTOGRAPHER **FRANK GREENAWAY**

Common octopus

Common
sunstar

DK | **Penguin Random House**

REVISED EDITION

DK LONDON
Senior Editor Carron Brown
Senior Art Editor Lynne Moulding
US Editor Kayla Dugger
US Executive Editor Lori Cates Hand
Managing Editor Francesca Baines
Managing Art Editor Philip Letsu
Production Editor Gillian Reid
Production Controller Samantha Cross
Jacket Design Development Manager Sophia MTT
Publisher Andrew Macintyre
Associate Publishing Director Liz Wheeler
Art Director Karen Self
Publishing Director Jonathan Metcalf

Consultant Stephen P. Savage

DK DELHI
Senior Editor Shatarupa Chaudhuri
Senior Art Editor Vikas Chauhan
Editor Avanika
Art Editor Tanisha Mandal
Picture Researcher Vishal Ghavri
Managing Editor Kingshuk Ghoshal
Managing Art Editor Govind Mittal
DTP Designers Pawan Kumar,
Nand Kishor Acharya, Rakesh Kumar
Jacket Designer Juhi Sheth

FIRST EDITION
Project Editor Marion Dent
Art Editor Jane Tetzlaff
Managing Editor Gillian Denton
Managing Art Editor Julia Harris
Research Céline Carez
Picture Research Kathy Lockley
Production Catherine Semark
Special thanks The University Marine Biological
Station (Scotland) and Sea Life Centres (UK)

This Eyewitness ® Book has been conceived by
Dorling Kindersley Limited and Editions Gallimard

This American Edition, 2021
First American Edition, 1995
Published in the United States by DK Publishing
1450 Broadway, Suite 801, New York, NY 10018

For the curious
www.dk.com

Microscope used
in the late 1800s

Prepared slides

Dead man's fingers

Parchment
worm inside
its tube

Red
cushion
star

Common
starfish

Mussel
shells

Red
cushion
star

Victorian
collection
of shells

Contents

Dahlia anemone

Oceans of the past

Today's oceans started to take shape in the last 200 million years of Earth's 4,600-million-year existence. But long before, as the early planet cooled, water vapor in the atmosphere condensed, clouds formed, and rain filled the oceans. Water also came from space in icy comets. As the land masses drifted, new oceans opened up, old oceans disappeared, and ocean life changed, too. Simple organisms first appeared in the oceans 3,500 million years ago, followed by ever more complex life forms.

Spine

Ridged scale

Topsy-turvy world
Wiwaxia lived on the sea floor 530 million years ago. Fossils have been found high above sea level in Canada's Rocky Mountains. Land formed under the sea was forced up to create mountain chains.

Strong belly ribs protected underside of bulky, rounded body

Femur, or thigh bone, articulated with pelvic girdle

All-around vision provided by large, curved eye

Front flipper also had five elongated toes

Short tail relative to total body length

Huge, long, flat flipper made up of five rows of elongated toes

Segmented body allowed trilobite to roll up like a woodlouse

Dead and gone
Once one of the most abundant creatures in ancient seas, trilobites flourished 510–250 million years ago. They had jointed limbs and an external skeleton like insects and crustaceans (such as crabs and lobsters).

Ancient coral

Corals were well preserved in rocks because of their hard skeletons, such as this 400-million-year-old fossil coral. Over the last 25 million years, the skeleton of each tiny coral animal joined that of its neighbor to create chains with spaces between them.

Most flexible vertebrae in neck

Long neck and small head typical of one type of plesiosaur

Arm used for moving and catching food

Sharp, interlocking teeth for capturing fish prey

Marine reptiles

Early reptiles mostly lived on land, but some of their descendants adapted to life in the sea. Plesiosaurs first appeared around 200 million years ago. They swam using their flippers as oars or wings to "fly" through water like turtles do today. They died out around 65 million years ago, about the same time as the dinosaurs. The only marine reptiles today are the sea snakes and sea turtles.

Ancient marine **sea lilies** are still found living below **330 ft (100 m).**

CHANGING EARTH

Fossil brittle star, *Palaeocoma*

Changing oceans

A giant ocean, Panthalassa, surrounded the supercontinent Pangea (1), 290–240 mya (million years ago). At the end of the period, many kinds of marine life became extinct. Pangea split apart, around the Tethys Sea.

Continental drift

The North Atlantic formed 208–146 mya (2). The South Atlantic and Indian Oceans began to form 146–65 mya (3). The continents continued to drift 1.64 mya (4), and the oceans are still changing shape today.

Still here today

This 180-million-year-old fossil brittle star looks like its living relative (above, left), which has five jointed arms that can easily break. It is often found on sandy or muddy sea beds.

Oceans today

All of Earth's seawater is linked in one continuous mass. The largest expanses are called oceans. Smaller ones (usually close to or partly enclosed by land) are called seas. Two-thirds of Earth's surface is covered by seawater, which makes up to 97 percent of the planet's entire water supply. The temperature of seawater is colder at the surface in polar regions than in the tropics and generally gets colder with depth. Salinity varies, too, as does the ocean floor—ranging from undersea mountains to plateaus, plains, and trenches.

God of the waters
Neptune, the Roman god of the sea, is often shown riding a dolphin and carrying a three-pronged spear (trident). He was also thought to control freshwater supplies.

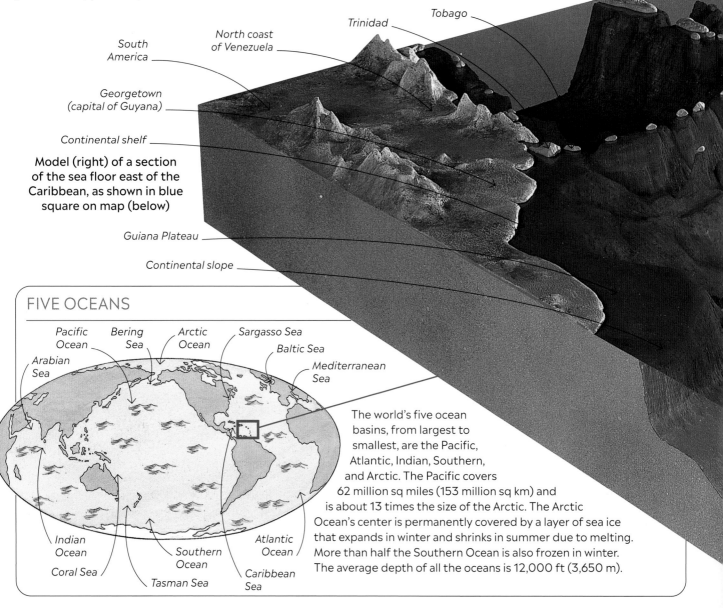

Haiti/Dominican Republic

Tobago

Trinidad

North coast of Venezuela

South America

Georgetown (capital of Guyana)

Continental shelf

Model (right) of a section of the sea floor east of the Caribbean, as shown in blue square on map (below)

Guiana Plateau

Continental slope

FIVE OCEANS

Pacific Ocean

Bering Sea

Arctic Ocean

Sargasso Sea

Baltic Sea

Arabian Sea

Mediterranean Sea

Indian Ocean

Coral Sea

Southern Ocean

Tasman Sea

Atlantic Ocean

Caribbean Sea

The world's five ocean basins, from largest to smallest, are the Pacific, Atlantic, Indian, Southern, and Arctic. The Pacific covers 62 million sq miles (153 million sq km) and is about 13 times the size of the Arctic. The Arctic Ocean's center is permanently covered by a layer of sea ice that expands in winter and shrinks in summer due to melting. More than half the Southern Ocean is also frozen in winter. The average depth of all the oceans is 12,000 ft (3,650 m).

DISAPPEARING ACT

The gigantic tectonic plates on Earth's crust move like a conveyor belt. New areas of ocean floor form at spreading centers, and old areas sink below trenches where one oceanic plate is forced under another (subduction).

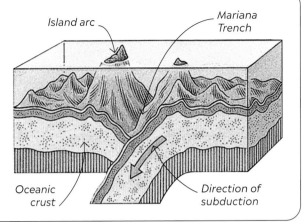

Island arc

Mariana Trench

Formation of Mariana Trench

Oceanic crust

Direction of subduction

EYEWITNESS

Wally Broecker
US geochemist Wally Broecker is a pioneer of paleoclimatology—the study of past climate changes. His research has uncovered the ocean circulating system, or the global ocean conveyor belt, in which warm surface water from the equator loses heat as it travels toward the Arctic, and this escaping heat forms Earth's climate.

The **Pacific Ocean** has the most number of islands in the world— **about 25,000.**

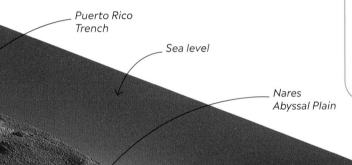

Hatteras Abyssal Plain

Puerto Rico Trench

Sea level

Nares Abyssal Plain

Mid-Atlantic Ridge

Kane Fracture Zone

Vema Fracture Zone

Demerara Abyssal Plain

The ocean floor

This model shows the Atlantic Ocean by northeast South America. Off this coast is the continental shelf, under relatively shallow water about 660 ft (200 m) deep. The shelf is about 125 miles (200 km) wide here, but it is up to 1,000 miles (1,600 km) wide off northern Asia. From there, the ocean floor drops steeply to form the continental slope. Sediments eroded from the land and carried by rivers accumulate at the bottom of this slope. The ocean floor then opens out in virtually flat abyssal plains. Deep trenches, such as the Puerto Rican Trench, can form where one of Earth's tectonic plates slides past another.

Ocean life

Oceans are home to some of the most diverse life on Earth. Animals live either on the sea bed or in midwater where they swim or float. Plants are only found in the sunlit zone and are anchored to the sea floor or drifting in the water. Animals are found at all depths but are most abundant in the sunlit zone where food is plentiful. Some animals move from one zone to another to surface for air or to find more food. More than 90 percent of all species dwell on the sea floor. One rock can house at least 10 major groups, such as corals and sponges.

TIME AND TIDE

Sun

Moon

Bulge due to gravitational pull of Moon and Sun

Bulge due to rotational force

Earth

Tides are caused by the gravitational pull of the Moon on Earth's seawater on one side of the planet and due to the same gravity pulling on Earth and Earth's own rotational force on the other. As Earth spins around over 24 hours, the bulges (high tides) usually occur twice a day in one place. The highest and lowest tides (spring tides) occur when Moon and Sun are in line.

THE OCEAN'S ZONES

The ocean is divided into zones. In the sunlit zone, there is plenty of light, water movement, and seasonal change in temperature. Beneath this is the twilight zone, with little light and temperatures that drop to about 41°F (5°C). Deeper yet is the dark zone, with no light and temperatures of about 34–36°F (1–2°C). Even deeper are zones on the sea bed, like the abyss and the trenches.

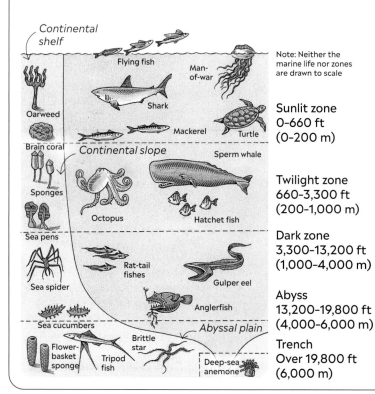

Continental shelf

Flying fish

Man-of-war

Note: Neither the marine life nor zones are drawn to scale

Oarweed

Shark

Mackerel

Turtle

Sunlit zone
0–660 ft
(0–200 m)

Brain coral

Continental slope

Sperm whale

Sponges

Octopus

Hatchet fish

Twilight zone
660–3,300 ft
(200–1,000 m)

Sea pens

Rat-tail fishes

Sea spider

Gulper eel

Dark zone
3,300–13,200 ft
(1,000–4,000 m)

Anglerfish

Sea cucumbers

Abyssal plain

Abyss
13,200–19,800 ft
(4,000–6,000 m)

Flower-basket sponge

Brittle star

Tripod fish

Deep-sea anemone

Trench
Over 19,800 ft
(6,000 m)

Green shore crab

Shore life

Often found on the shore at low tide, starfish also live in deeper water. Sea life on the shore must either be tough enough to withstand drying out or shelter in rock pools.

Common sunstar

Inside squid's soft body is a horny, penlike shell

Funnel expels jet of water for moving in sea

Tentacles reach out to grasp food

Speedy squid

One of the most common animals in the sea, squid often swim in shoals for protection. Built like streamlined torpedoes, they can swim quickly.

Magnificent weed

Growing on the sea bed, the giant kelp has a central, stemlike stalk, with leaflike blades. Each blade has a gas-filled air bladder, which keeps the kelp afloat. Spreading out its blades, it absorbs sunshine for making food by photosynthesis. Giant kelps grow over 1 ft (0.3 m) a day. Off North America's Pacific coast, kelp forests provide a home for many species, including fishes, sea otters, and sea urchins.

Deep-sea shark

Many people think of sharks as dangerous predators, but like most sharks, this cat shark from the deep Pacific Ocean is harmless. Some bony fishes have gas-filled air bladders to stop them from sinking, but sharks have oil-rich livers instead.

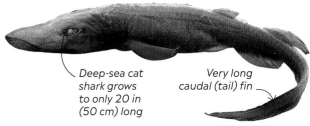

Deep-sea cat shark grows to only 20 in (50 cm) long

Very long caudal (tail) fin

Long tentacles catch food drifting by in sea

Sea fir's stem grows out of muddy sand

Sea firs

In 1985, living specimens of sea firs were first observed from a submersible craft. The sea fir catches food drifting by in its long tentacles and can even tackle tiny fishes up to 1 in (2 cm) long. It is found in the Pacific Ocean at 165–17,500 ft (50–5,300 m) and in the Atlantic Ocean.

Icy ocean

There are two main types of sea ice: pack ice on the open sea (above) and fast ice between land and pack ice. Being salty, seawater freezes at lower temperatures than fresh water. As ice forms on top, the salt is forced into the water just below, causing it to sink by making it heavier. Surface seawater flows in to replace the sinking water, powering the global ocean conveyor belt (see p.9). Icebergs are huge chunks broken off polar ice sheets and glaciers.

Waves and weather

Seawater is always moving. Winds drive the waves and major surface currents are driven by the prevailing winds. Surface and deep-water currents help modify the world's climate by moving cold water from polar regions toward the tropics and vice versa. Heat from the oceans creates air movement. The ocean heats up more slowly than the land by day. Cool air above the water blows in, replacing warm air above the land, and the reverse at night.

Rain falls on land

Water from land flows into ocean (runoff)

Rive

Water is absorbed into soil

Groundwater seeps back

Day 2: Thunderstorms as swirling cloud mass

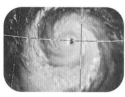

Day 4: Winds have increased in intensity

Day 7: Strong winds

A hurricane is born

These satellite images show a hurricane forming, from a swirling cloud mass to ferocious winds over seven days.

RIVERS OF THE SEA

Currents are huge masses of water moving through the oceans. The course that currents follow is not precisely the same as the trade winds and westerlies, because currents are deflected by land and the Coriolis Force produced by Earth's rotation. The latter causes currents to shift to the right in the northern hemisphere and to the left in the southern.

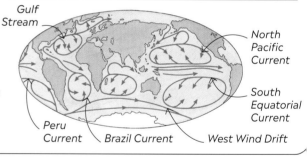

Gulf Stream

North Pacific Current

South Equatorial Current

Peru Current

Brazil Current

West Wind Drift

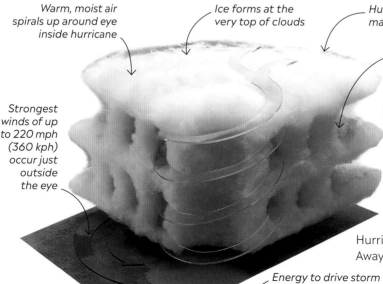

Warm, moist air spirals up around eye inside hurricane

Ice forms at the very top of clouds

Hurricanes are enormous—some may be 500 miles (800 km) across

Torrential rains fall from clouds

Strongest winds of up to 220 mph (360 kph) occur just outside the eye

Energy to drive storm comes from a warm ocean at 80°F (27°C) or more

Hurricane!

Also known as typhoons, hurricanes form in the tropics where warm, moist air rises up from the ocean's surface, creating storm clouds. As more air spirals upward, the energy released fuels stronger winds that whirl around the eye (a calm area of extreme low pressure). Hurricanes cause devastation over land. Away from the ocean, they die out.

Water cycle

Water is constantly moving between land, river, ocean, and air in what is called the water cycle. The Sun heats up the water, causing it to evaporate into water vapor. As it rises, the water vapor cools, condenses into water droplets, and falls back on Earth as precipitation in the form of rain, snow, or hail. This water seeps into the land and flows back to the sea.

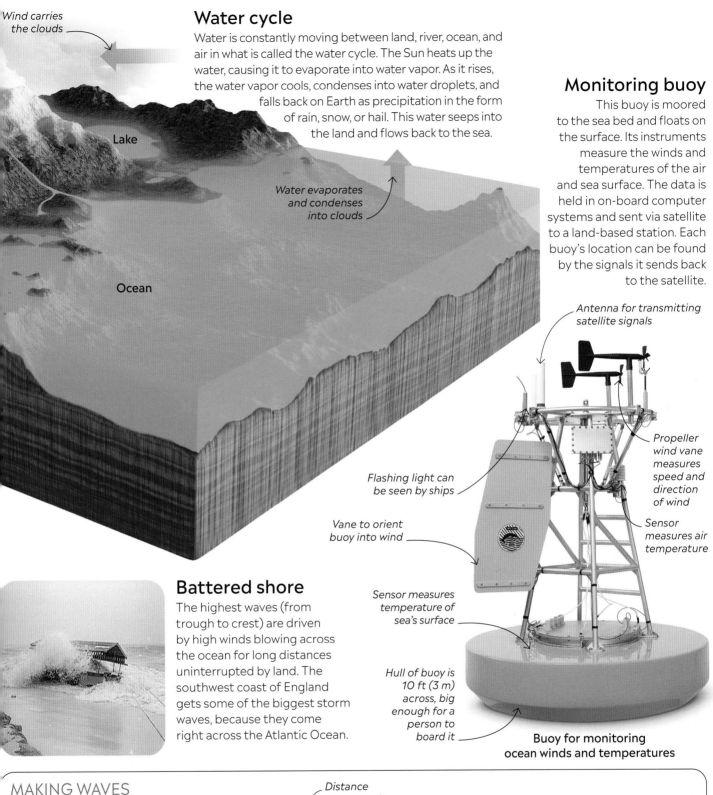

Wind carries the clouds

Lake

Water evaporates and condenses into clouds

Ocean

Monitoring buoy

This buoy is moored to the sea bed and floats on the surface. Its instruments measure the winds and temperatures of the air and sea surface. The data is held in on-board computer systems and sent via satellite to a land-based station. Each buoy's location can be found by the signals it sends back to the satellite.

Antenna for transmitting satellite signals

Propeller wind vane measures speed and direction of wind

Flashing light can be seen by ships

Sensor measures air temperature

Vane to orient buoy into wind

Sensor measures temperature of sea's surface

Hull of buoy is 10 ft (3 m) across, big enough for a person to board it

Buoy for monitoring ocean winds and temperatures

Battered shore

The highest waves (from trough to crest) are driven by high winds blowing across the ocean for long distances uninterrupted by land. The southwest coast of England gets some of the biggest storm waves, because they come right across the Atlantic Ocean.

MAKING WAVES

Waves are formed by wind on the surface of water, causing friction. Wind energy shifts to the water and travels as a wave, which moves forward in the same direction as the wind, but the water barely shifts at all. It follows a circular path, shown by the bottle. Waves driven toward a beach break when the water becomes too shallow and the energy is let out on the shore.

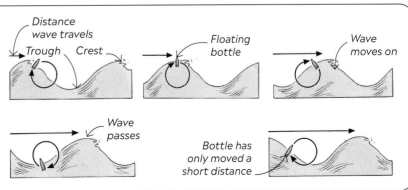

Distance wave travels

Trough *Crest*

Floating bottle

Wave moves on

Wave passes

Bottle has only moved a short distance

Sandy and muddy

In some shallow coastal waters, the sea bed is covered in sand or organic mud that has eroded from rocks, washed from the land, or been deposited by rivers. Here, vast stretches of the sea floor look like underwater deserts. Finer-grained mud settles in places where the water is calmer. Without rocks, there are few places to hide, so animals that venture onto the surface are exposed to predators. Many of these creatures avoid danger by hiding in the soft sea bed. All the animals shown here live in the coastal waters of the Atlantic Ocean.

Coarse, shiny bristles help it move along sea bed

Bulky body 4 in (10 cm) long is covered by dense mat of fine hairs

Bristling beauty

The sea mouse plows through muddy sand on the sea bed, hunting small worms and eating any dead animals it finds. The rainbow-colored spines help propel this chunky worm and may deter hungry fish. Keeping its rear end out of the sand brings in fresh seawater to help it breathe.

Poisonous spines on first dorsal fin

High-set eye allows all-around vision

Poisonous spine on front of gill cover

Upturned mouth grabs prey from beneath the sand

Tentacles disappear fast into tube if danger is present

Wary weever

When a weever fish is buried in sand, the eyes on top of its head help it see what is going on. Poisonous spines provide extra defense and can inflict nasty wounds if a weever is trodden on or caught in a fishing net.

Shark science specialist
Shark biologist Samuel H. Gruber (1938–2019) studied lemon sharks—a species that swims close to the sandy sea bed in shallow coastal waters—for years. His research found that these sharks had amazing eyesight and that each shark studied had its own character traits and level of intelligence.

Tentacles fringed with fine hairs

Flat fish

Flounders cruise along the sea bed looking for food. They feed on small fish and crustaceans and even nibble the tops off peacock worms. They swim on their side and can change color to hide in the sand.

Flat body

Peacock worm can be 10 in (25 cm) long

Like a peacock's fan

A crown of tentacles helps peacock worms feed and breathe. As water passes through the tentacles, particles in the water are passed down rows of tiny beating hairs into the mouth in the crown's center. Larger particles help make the tube.

Tube made of mud and sand particles bound together with worm's hardened slime

Soft sea bed

On a soft sea bed, few animals are visible, because most of them live buried in the sand. You may spot a crab's feathery antennae or a clam's siphon, which help these animals get a clean supply of oxygenated water to breathe. Some fish visit the soft sea bed to feed on burrowing clams. Other animals are found among sea grasses. These flowering plants are food for many animals.

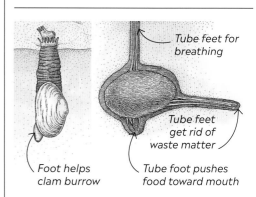
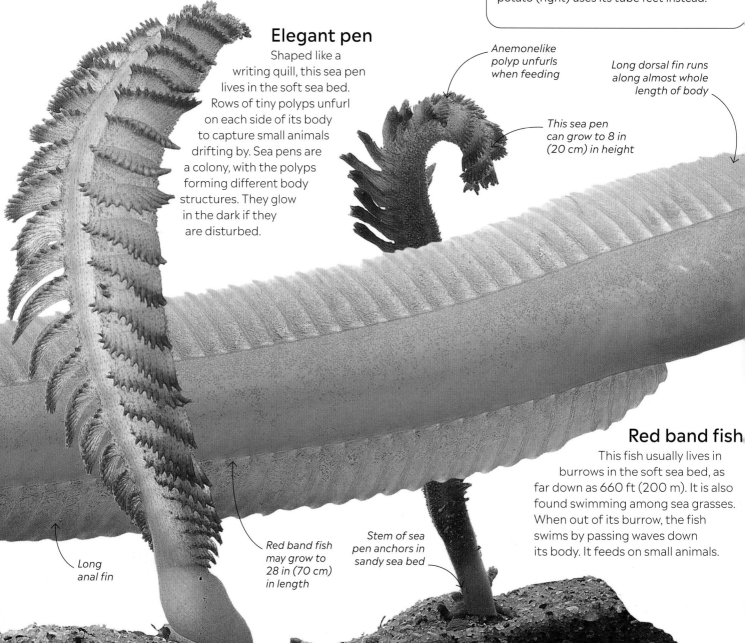

Elegant pen
Shaped like a writing quill, this sea pen lives in the soft sea bed. Rows of tiny polyps unfurl on each side of its body to capture small animals drifting by. Sea pens are a colony, with the polyps forming different body structures. They glow in the dark if they are disturbed.

Anemonelike polyp unfurls when feeding

Long dorsal fin runs along almost whole length of body

This sea pen can grow to 8 in (20 cm) in height

Red band fish
This fish usually lives in burrows in the soft sea bed, as far down as 660 ft (200 m). It is also found swimming among sea grasses. When out of its burrow, the fish swims by passing waves down its body. It feeds on small animals.

Long anal fin

Red band fish may grow to 28 in (70 cm) in length

Stem of sea pen anchors in sandy sea bed

Masked crab

By day, this crab hides in the sand, with only its two antennae sticking out. These feelers link to form a breathing tube when the crab is buried. Water passes down the tube and over the crab's gills. At night, the crab comes out to find food, such as small shrimp.

Front claw, or pincer

Crab's antennae linked together by bristles

Facelike markings on shell give crab its name

Back leg used for digging

Seahorse can be up to 5 in (12 cm) long

Horselike head

Dorsal fin beats 20 to 35 times per second

Seahorse uncurls tail to rise up in water

Handy tail

Seahorses are usually found among corals, sea grasses, or seaweeds. Unlike most fish, they swim with their bodies upright and move by waves passing down their dorsal fin. They feed on small animals, sucking them into their mouths.

Tail curls around seaweed

Large eye helps spot prey

Pectoral fin, or wing

Short pectoral fin

Bulgy, fleshy head

Pointed snout

Bat eagle ray can grow up to 5.9 ft (1.8 m)

Eagle ray

The bat eagle ray flaps its two large, winglike pectoral fins as it swims along the sea bed. It searches out shellfish with its snout and crushes them between bands of flattened teeth. Eagle rays can leap right out of the water.

Rocks underwater

The sea bed in some coastal waters is rocky where currents sweep away any sand and mud. To survive, animals must cling onto rocks, find crevices to hide in, or shelter in seaweeds. Piddocks (clams) and some sea urchins can bore into soft rock to make their homes. Some animals hide under small stones lodged in the soft sea bed or attach themselves to its surface, but where masses of loose pebbles roll around, animals and seaweeds would be crushed. Other animals can survive at the water's edge, especially in rock pools, but many need to stay submerged.

Sea urchin boring into rocks

Piddock

Rock borers

Some sea urchins use their spines and teeth to bore holes in rock. Using its muscular foot, the piddock twists and turns to drill with the ridges on the edge of the tip of its shell where it will live.

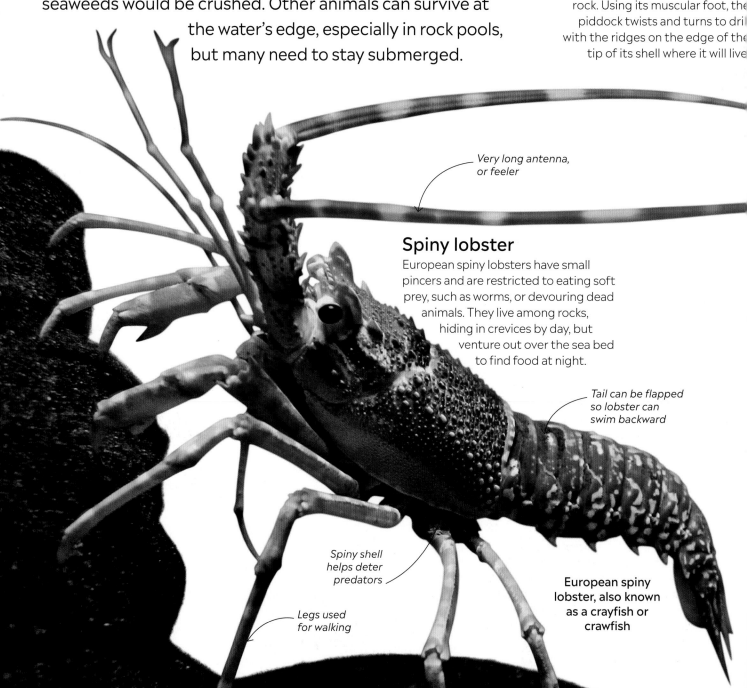

Very long antenna, or feeler

Spiny lobster

European spiny lobsters have small pincers and are restricted to eating soft prey, such as worms, or devouring dead animals. They live among rocks, hiding in crevices by day, but venture out over the sea bed to find food at night.

Tail can be flapped so lobster can swim backward

Spiny shell helps deter predators

Legs used for walking

European spiny lobster, also known as a crayfish or crawfish

Monster claws

The savage sea monster in this old engraving looks like a lobster with two giant-sized pincers. Real lobsters can grow to 35 in (90 cm) long and weigh up to 44 lb (20 kg).

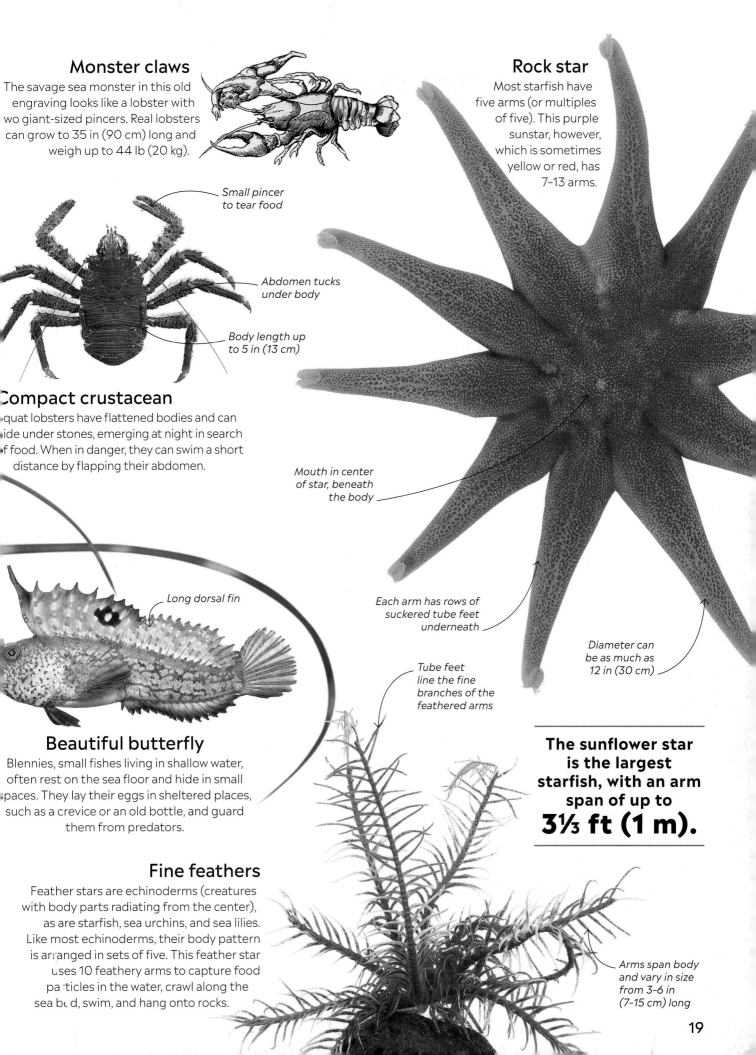

Small pincer to tear food

Abdomen tucks under body

Body length up to 5 in (13 cm)

Compact crustacean

Squat lobsters have flattened bodies and can hide under stones, emerging at night in search of food. When in danger, they can swim a short distance by flapping their abdomen.

Rock star

Most starfish have five arms (or multiples of five). This purple sunstar, however, which is sometimes yellow or red, has 7–13 arms.

Mouth in center of star, beneath the body

Each arm has rows of suckered tube feet underneath

Diameter can be as much as 12 in (30 cm)

Long dorsal fin

Beautiful butterfly

Blennies, small fishes living in shallow water, often rest on the sea floor and hide in small spaces. They lay their eggs in sheltered places, such as a crevice or an old bottle, and guard them from predators.

Tube feet line the fine branches of the feathered arms

The sunflower star is the largest starfish, with an arm span of up to 3⅓ ft (1 m).

Fine feathers

Feather stars are echinoderms (creatures with body parts radiating from the center), as are starfish, sea urchins, and sea lilies. Like most echinoderms, their body pattern is arranged in sets of five. This feather star uses 10 feathery arms to capture food particles in the water, crawl along the sea bed, swim, and hang onto rocks.

Arms span body and vary in size from 3–6 in (7–15 cm) long

On the rocks

In shallow, cool waters above rocky sea beds, forests of kelp (large brown seaweeds) are home to many sea creatures. Fish swim among the giant fronds. Sea otters wrap themselves in giant kelp while sleeping on the surface. Tightly gripping the rocks, the kelp's rootlike anchor (holdfast) houses many tiny creatures, such as crabs, worms, sea squirts, and sponges. Anchored to rocks, mussels provide homes for some animals between or within their shells.

Sharp-tipped claw for hanging onto seaweed

Long legs

The long-legged, aptly named spider crab hides under rocks and among seaweeds on the lower shore and in shallow waters, hanging on with its claws. To blend in, it plucks bits of seaweed with its pincers and attaches them to its shell.

Seaweed on legs as part of camouflage

Scaleless body is covered with small, warty bumps

Hold on tight

Lumpsuckers, or lumpfish, cling to rocks with suckerlike fins on their bellies. They come into shallow water to breed, and the father guards the eggs.

Juvenile lumpsucker

Each sturdy, blunt finger measures at least 1 in (3 cm) across

Anchored algae

Holdfasts of the large, tough, brown algae called kelp keep it firmly anchored to the rocks.

Fleshy fingers supported by many tiny, hard splinters

Holdfast of oarweed kelp

Dead man's fingers

Growing on rocks, the colonies of this soft coral consist of individual small animals (polyps) within a fleshy orange or white skeleton.

White, anemonelike polyp captures food from fast currents

Gills

Holdfast must be strong, as some kinds of kelp can grow tens of feet long

Microscopic sea mat

The lacy-looking growth on the kelp's surface is a colony of bryozoans, or moss animals. Each little compartment houses one of these animals, which come out to capture food in their tiny tentacles. Other kinds of moss animals grow upward, looking like seaweeds or corals. Here, between the sea mats, is a blue-rayed limpet.

Sea slug

Many sea slugs are carnivorous. This slug lives on the soft coral known as dead man's fingers. Sea slug eggs hatch into swimming young, which then settle and turn into adults.

Help our kelp

Marine biologist Nancy Caruso and her team dived into the waters of Orange County, CA, with thousands of tiny kelp plants to attach them to the ocean floor. She helps revive kelp forest ecosystems known as the rainforests of the ocean.

Pea crab may nibble mussel's gills

Seaweeds growing on mussel shell

Horse mussel and pea crab

Heavy-shelled horse mussels live in colonies on rocks or kelp holdfasts in shallow water. The pea crab lives within the shell, feeding on the mussel's food, which can stunt the growth of the mussel. The pea crab enters the shell in its larval form.

Horse mussel grows to 8 in (20 cm) long

Feathery tentacles held on tough, single stems

Anemonelike polyp with two rings of tentacles to capture food

Sea flowers

This sea fir (hydroid) looks a bit like a flowering plant, but it belongs to the same group of animals as corals, jellyfish, and sea anemones. Sea firs grow attached to surfaces, such as rocks and seaweeds, with branching out colonies of anemonelike polyps. These have tentacles that are used to capture food particles carried past in the current. If disturbed, the sea fir will withdraw its polyps into its horny skeleton.

Sea mat growing on surface

The coral
kingdom

In tropical waters, coral reefs cover vast areas. Most stony corals are colonies of many tiny, anemonelike polyps. Each one makes a hard limestone cup (skeleton) that protects its soft body. They do this with the help of microscopic, single-celled algae that live inside them. The algae need sunlight to grow, so coral reefs are found only in sunny surface waters. Only the upper layer of a reef is made of living corals, which build upon skeletons of dead polyps.

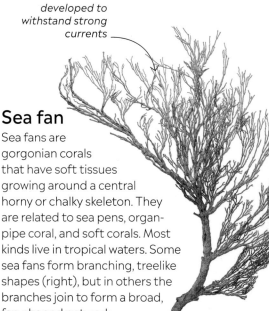

INSIDE A CORAL

Polyps are linked by a layer of tissue to share nutrients. To reproduce, they divide in two or release eggs and sperm.

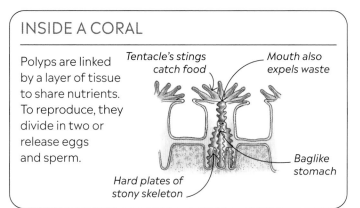

Tentacle's stings catch food

Mouth also expels waste

Baglike stomach

Hard plates of stony skeleton

Brain coral's convoluted surface looks like that of a human brain

Stone brain
The surface of living brain coral is covered with soft tissue. Anemonelike polyps grow in rows along the channels in this slow-growing, stony coral's skeleton.

Stinging coral
Colorful hydrocorals are related to sea firs. Known as fire corals, they have potent stings on their polyps.

Staghorn coral
This important reef-building coral grows about 4 in (10 cm) in a year. Its antlerlike shape allows lots of water and food to flow around its skeleton.

Intricate mesh developed to withstand strong currents

Sea fan
Sea fans are gorgonian corals that have soft tissues growing around a central horny or chalky skeleton. They are related to sea pens, organ-pipe coral, and soft corals. Most kinds live in tropical waters. Some sea fans form branching, treelike shapes (right), but in others the branches join to form a broad, fan-shaped network.

Biggest and best

More than 1,200 miles (2,000 km) long, Australia's Great Barrier Reef is the largest structure in the world made by living organisms. It is thousands of years old and includes 400 kinds of hard coral; 1,625 species of fish; and 4,300 species of crustacean and mollusk.

Black coral

In living black corals, the skeleton provides support for the living tissues and the branches bear rows of anemonelike polyps. Mainly tropical, it grows in the deep part of coral reefs.

Black coral's horny skeleton looks like a bunch of twigs

Queen scallops living within the rose coral's folds

Organ pipes

In living organ-pipe coral, anemonelike polyps emerge from the bright-red skeleton's tiny pipes. This is not a true stony coral, but a relative of sea fans, soft coral, and sea pens.

A coral by any other name

Rose coral is a moss animal, growing on the sea bed in colonies made of millions of tiny animals.

ATOLL IN THE MAKING

An atoll is a ring of coral islands around a central lagoon. Charles Darwin (1809–1882) realized they grew around a volcanic island, which then sank.

Fringing reef grows around volcano

As volcano subsides, lagoon appears, creating barrier reef

Volcano disappears, leaving behind coral atoll

23

Life on a **coral reef**

Coral reefs support an amazing variety of marine life. Every bit of space gives shelter to some animal or plant. At night, a host of different creatures emerges from coral caves and crevices to feed, though some are active in the day. They all depend on the stony corals that recycle scarce nutrients from the tropical waters. People, as well as animals, rely on coral reefs as they protect coastlines, and some island nations live on coral atolls. Sadly, coral reefs are under threat, damaged by snorkelers and divers treading on them, dynamited by fishermen, and polluted by sewage and oil spills.

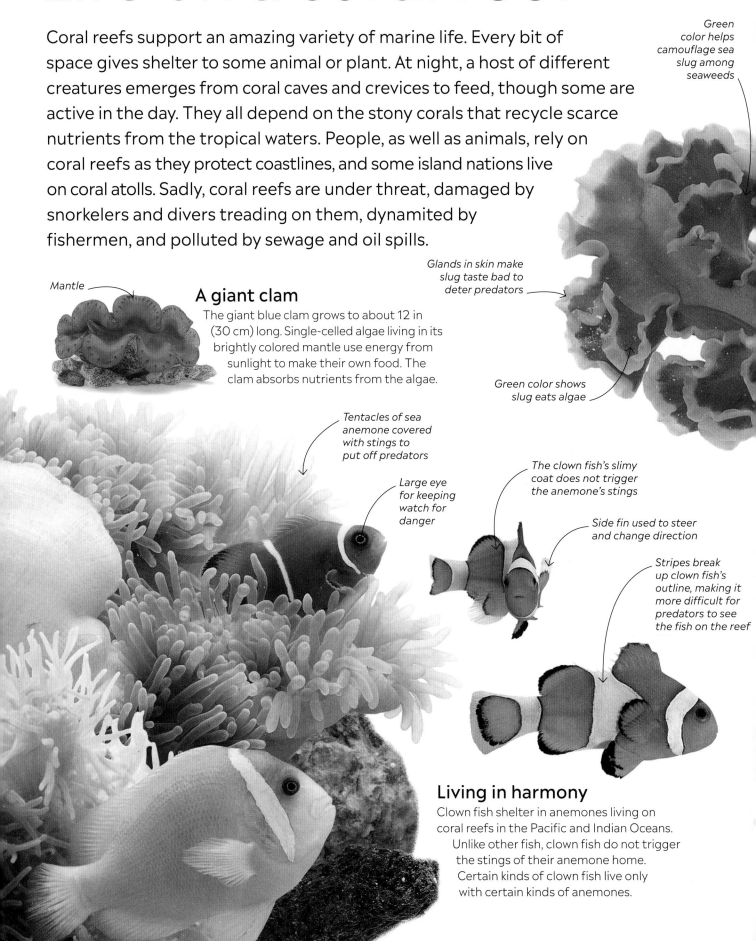

Green color helps camouflage sea slug among seaweeds

Mantle

A giant clam

The giant blue clam grows to about 12 in (30 cm) long. Single-celled algae living in its brightly colored mantle use energy from sunlight to make their own food. The clam absorbs nutrients from the algae.

Glands in skin make slug taste bad to deter predators

Green color shows slug eats algae

Tentacles of sea anemone covered with stings to put off predators

Large eye for keeping watch for danger

The clown fish's slimy coat does not trigger the anemone's stings

Side fin used to steer and change direction

Stripes break up clown fish's outline, making it more difficult for predators to see the fish on the reef

Living in harmony

Clown fish shelter in anemones living on coral reefs in the Pacific and Indian Oceans. Unlike other fish, clown fish do not trigger the stings of their anemone home. Certain kinds of clown fish live only with certain kinds of anemones.

Date mussel

This date mussel makes its home by producing chemicals to wear a hole in the hard coral. It filters food particles from water passing through its gills.

Adult

Adult's colors and patterns act as signals to other angelfish and help attract a mate

Juvenile

Ring patterns may draw predator away from juvenile's more vulnerable head

Narrow snout probes rocks for sponges and other animals

Growing up

The young emperor angelfish looks different from the adult, and its colors may protect it better. Once adults pair up and establish territories on the reef, their colors and patterns help other emperors recognize them and keep off their patch.

Soft body has no shell to protect slug

Lettuce slug breathes through its leafy-looking skin

EYEWITNESS

Saving reefs

The Coral Restoration Foundation (CRF) works extensively to restore coral reefs. It grows different coral species in ocean nurseries and replants them in reefs to revive them. Here, the founder of the CRF, Ken Nedimyer, is tending coral in a nursery.

Notorious starfish

The crown-of-thorns starfish eats coral polyps and can wreck a coral reef. Like many other starfish, it turns its stomach inside out, making enzymes to digest its prey. Its main predator is the triton sea snail.

Frilly lettuce

Sea slugs are related to sea snails but do not have shells. Many feed on the coral, but the lettuce slug feeds on algae growing on the reef by sucking the sap from their cells. Stored in the slug's digestive system, chloroplasts—the green parts of plant cells—continue to trap energy from sunlight to make food.

Tentacles around mouth used for feeding

One of five rows of tube feet that help sea cucumber crawl

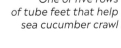

Colorful cucumber

This colorful sea cucumber lives on or close to reefs in the Indo-Pacific region. Sea cucumbers are echinoderms (p. 19), like starfish, sea urchins, and sea lilies. Sea cucumbers put out sticky tentacles to catch small particles of food and put them in their mouth.

Special fat tentacles for smelling food

Sea meadows

The most abundant plants in the ocean are minute floating plants called phytoplankton. Like all plants, they need sunlight to grow and live in the ocean's upper zone. Light is most abundant in the tropics, but nutrients are in short supply here. Huge phytoplankton blooms are found in cooler waters where nutrients (dead plant and animal waste) are brought up from the bottom during storms and in both cool and warm waters where there are upwellings of nutrient-rich water. Phytoplankton are mostly eaten by tiny animals (zooplankton); some of the biggest fish and whales feed directly on zooplankton.

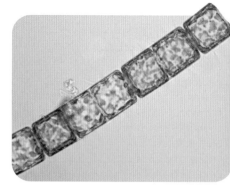

Plant food

This diatom is one of many phytoplankton that drift in the ocean. Many diatoms are single cells, but this one consists of a chain of cells. Phytoplankton release as much oxygen as forests and land plants.

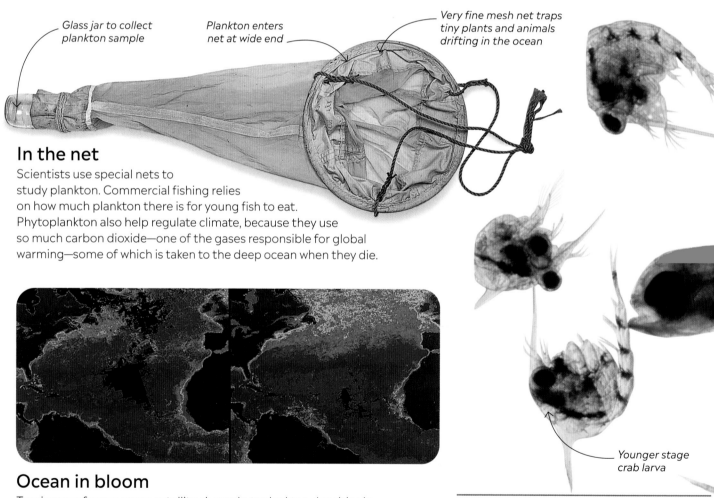

Glass jar to collect plankton sample

Plankton enters net at wide end

Very fine mesh net traps tiny plants and animals drifting in the ocean

In the net

Scientists use special nets to study plankton. Commercial fishing relies on how much plankton there is for young fish to eat. Phytoplankton also help regulate climate, because they use so much carbon dioxide—one of the gases responsible for global warming—some of which is taken to the deep ocean when they die.

Younger stage crab larva

Ocean in bloom

Two images from a space satellite show phytoplankton densities in the Atlantic Ocean. Red shows where phytoplankton are densest through yellow; green; blue; to violet, where it is least dense. Phytoplankton's spring bloom (right) occurs when days are longer and more nutrients come up from the bottom. A second, smaller bloom occurs in the fall (left).

Most phytoplankton live in the top 656 ft (200 m) of the ocean.

FOOD CHAINS

Plankton is at the bottom of the food chains. Phytoplankton are mostly eaten by zooplankton, which are eaten by small fish, which in turn are eaten by larger fish. These big fish provide food for large predators such as seals, whales, and polar bears.

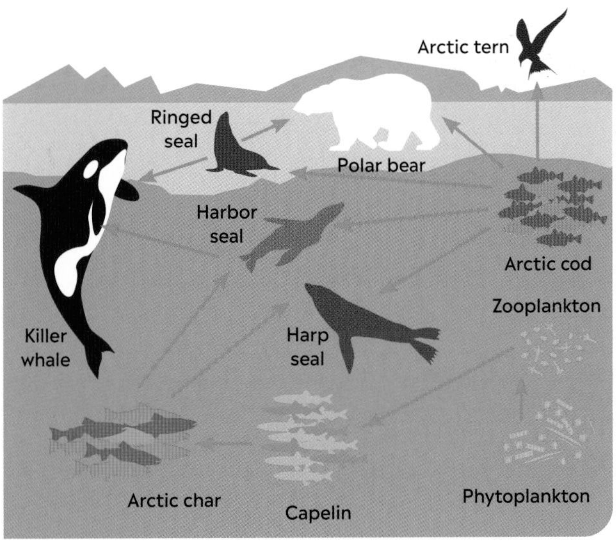

Arctic tern

Ringed seal

Polar bear

Harbor seal

Killer whale

Harp seal

Arctic cod

Zooplankton

Arctic char

Capelin

Phytoplankton

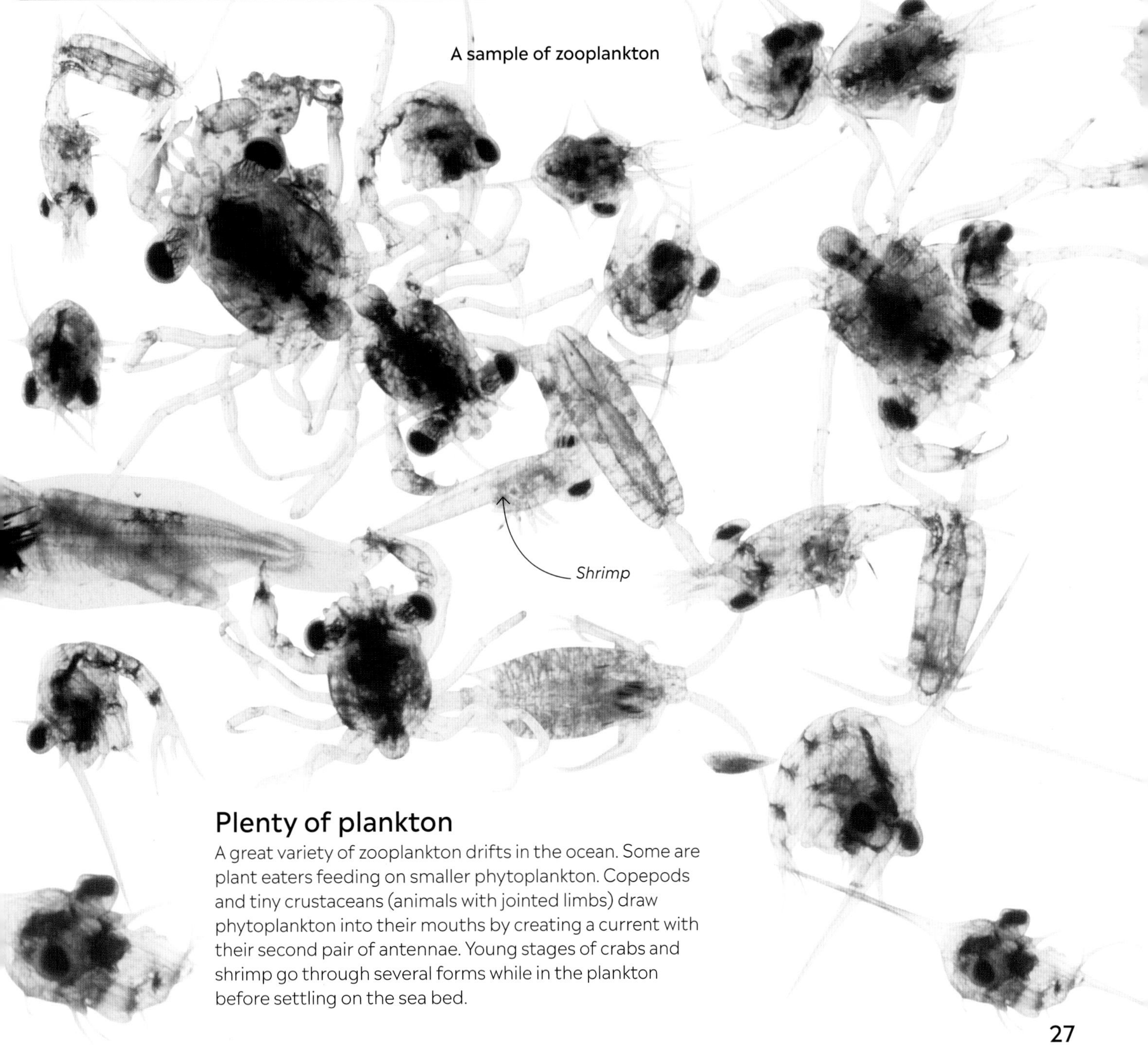

Young fish

A sample of zooplankton

Shrimp

Plenty of plankton

A great variety of zooplankton drifts in the ocean. Some are plant eaters feeding on smaller phytoplankton. Copepods and tiny crustaceans (animals with jointed limbs) draw phytoplankton into their mouths by creating a current with their second pair of antennae. Young stages of crabs and shrimp go through several forms while in the plankton before settling on the sea bed.

Predators

Some ocean animals are herbivores (plant eaters), which feed on seaweeds or phytoplankton. There are also many carnivores (meat eaters), large and small. Some are swift hunters; others set traps for their prey, waiting to attack with snapping jaws or stinging tentacles. Many animals strain food out of the water, and seabirds dive for a beakful of prey. Omnivores eat both plants and animals.

Cooperative feeding

Humpback whales encircle a shoal of fish, gulp in water and food, then expe the water through sievelike baleer plates in their mouths

Fang face

The wolf fish has strong, fanglike teeth that crunch through the hard shells of crabs, sea urchins, and mussels. As the front set is worn down each year or broken, it is replaced by a new set growing behind.

Tiny prey caught in mucus

Caught by slime

Many jellyfish sting their prey, but the common jellyfish traps tiny plankton in mucus from its bell. Four arms collect up the food-laden slime and tiny hairlike cilia channel it into the mouth.

Dorsal fin runs along entire length of body

Crooked, yellow, fanglike teeth

Pectoral fin

Tough, wrinkled skin helps protect wolf fish living near the sea bed

Tiger shark

Pelican diving

Pouchlike beak

Tiny teeth of a basking shark

Tiger shark's tooth

To bite or not to bite

A tiger shark's pointed, serrated teeth can pierce and slice through almost anything, from hard-shelled turtles to seals and seabirds. A basking shark's rows of tiny teeth are not used at all—it filters food from water with a sieve of gill rakers.

Feeding on fishes

Like all pelicans, the brown pelican has a big beak with a large pouch of skin to capture fish. Only brown pelicans dive far below the surface for their prey. When the pelican surfaces, it drains the water from its pouch and swallows the fish.

Stinging tentacle

Any undigested pieces of food are ejected through the mouth

Muscular disk lets Dahlia anemone attach to any hard surface

Tentacle traps

Flowerlike Dahlia anemones are deadly traps for shrimp and small fish that brush past the tentacles. Hundreds of nematocysts (stinging cells) fire their stings, and the tentacles pass the stricken prey to the mouth in the center—the entrance to the baglike stomach.

Homes and hiding

Staying hidden is one of the best means of defense—if a predator cannot see you, it is less likely to eat you! Many sea animals shelter among seaweeds, in crevices, or under the sand. Camouflage matching the background also helps sea creatures remain hidden. The sargassum fish even looks like bits of seaweed. Hard shells give protection from weak-jawed predators. Sea snails and clams make their own shells to cover the body, while crabs and lobsters have outer shells, like suits of armor, covering the body and each jointed limb.

What a weed

This fish lives among floating clumps of sargassum seaweed, where frilly growths on its head, body, and fins help it avoid being seen by predators, making a realistic disguise.

Blending in

Cuttlefish have different-colored pigments and rapidly change color to escape predators. The brain signals tiny bags of pigment in a cuttlefish's skin to contract, making the animal look paler.

Cuttlefish becomes darker when pigment bags expand

Hermit crab leaving old whelk shell

Anemone

When out of its shell, the crab is vulnerable to predators

Investigating its new home by checking size with its claws

Hermit crab moves into a perspex shell

All change

Hermit crabs lack armor around their abdomen, so they live in the empty shells of sea snails and other creatures. A hermit crab grows by shedding its hard, outer skeleton in the safety of its shell home. As it grows larger, it looks for a bigger shell to move into. When it finds one that is right, it pulls its body out of the old shell, tucking it quickly into the new one.

Leg with pointed claws to get a grip on sea bed when walking

Antenna

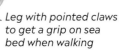

Shells on shells

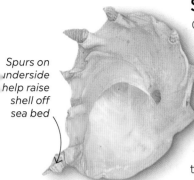

Spurs on underside help raise shell off sea bed

Carrier shells are sea snails that attach empty shells and bits of coral, stone, and broken glass to their own shells. This debris is a disguise against predators such as fish. It may also make it more difficult for fish to crack open the shell to reach the soft meat inside.

Remora fish attach themselves to sharks with a special sucker to **travel safely** in open waters.

Decorating shells

Some sea animals disguise their bodies by attaching bits of seaweed and debris to their shells to hide from predators. Decorator crabs, such as the one shown above, go a step further by adding sedentary or immobile animals such as sea anemones to their shells, as their stinging tentacles provide extra protection.

Crab's soft body winds around shell's spirals

Large pincer, or cheliped, used to block entrance to shell, providing extra security, and also to pick up food

Home sweet home

The European hermit crab first makes its home in smaller shells, such as a periwinkle shell or topshell, which it finds on the shore. When the crab grows larger, it usually lives in whelk shells. Hermit crabs carry their homes around with them and the females rear the eggs inside their shells.

Attack and defense

Many sea creatures have weapons to attack prey or defend themselves from predators. Some produce venom (poison) for defense and often warn of their danger with markings. The lionfish's stripes may alert enemies to its venomous spines, but being easy to see, it hunts at dusk, when it can surprise prey. Disappearing behind a cloud of ink is a useful trick used by octopuses, squid, and cuttlefish. But no defense method is foolproof, as even the most venomous jellyfish can be eaten by carnivorous turtles that are immune to their stings.

Deadly stonefish
Never tread on a stonefish. Sharp spines on its back inject a venom that causes such pain that the shock can kill.

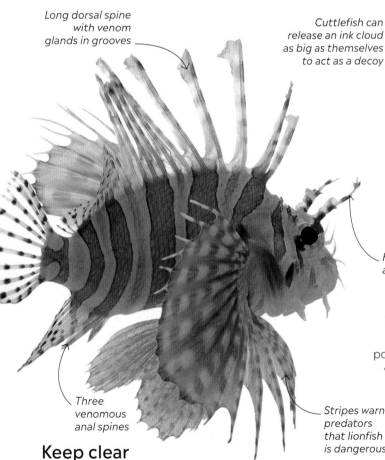

Long dorsal spine with venom glands in grooves

Cuttlefish can release an ink cloud as big as themselves to act as a decoy

Ink screen
Cephalopods (squid, cuttlefish, and octopuses) produce a cloud of ink to confuse an enemy and allow time to flee. The ink is ejected in a jet of water from a tubelike funnel near the head.

Horny projection above eye

Blue for danger
If this octopus senses danger, blue-ringed spots appear on its skin, warning of its poisonous bite. Living in shallow, often tropical waters, this blue-ringed octopus is the size of your hand, but its bite can be fatal.

Three venomous anal spines

Stripes warn predators that lionfish is dangerous

Keep clear
A predator ignoring the warning coloration and trying to bite a striped lionfish may be impaled by one or more of its poisonous spines. Lionfish have very few natural predators, such as sharks, groupers, and large eels, and are generally able to survive well.

Maerl (a chalky, red seaweed) grows in a thick mass along the stony sea bed

Stinger in the tail

This blue-spotted ray lives in warm waters and is often found lurking on the sandy sea bed. The stinger can be used for defense, but the ray is most likely to swim off at speed.

Two venomous spines on tail can pierce the swimmer's skin and inject venom

Stingray's stinger is sharp and serrated, easily piercing the skin

Pectoral fin used for swimming

Painting of sea monsters, c.1880s

Something scary

Early sailors knew that some creatures of the deep were deadly. As there was little knowledge of sea life, they told exaggerated tales about sea monsters and made them up to account for ships lost at sea.

Jellyfish

Jellyfish are known for their stings, but the nastiest stings are those of the box jellyfish in the Pacific Ocean. They produce welts on anyone who comes in contact with their tentacles. A badly stung person can die in four minutes.

When shell is closed, there is still a gap between the shell's two halves

Shaggy shells

These gaping file shells cannot pull their orange tentacles inside the two halves of their shell for protection, so the tentacles produce a sticky, sour-tasting substance to deter predators. Gaping file shells also put out silky threads for anchorage. If dislodged, they can move by expelling water from their shell and using their tentacles like oars.

Shell is up to 1 in (2.5 cm) long

The jet set

One way to swim quickly and escape from predators is by jet propulsion. Some mollusks, such as clams, squid, and octopuses, do this by squirting water from the body cavity. Squid are best at this—their bodies are streamlined to reduce drag (resistance to water). Some kinds of scallops also use jet propulsion and are among the few clams that can swim. If attacked, the common octopus uses this same technique to jet off.

Jet propulsion

The engines powering a jet plane produce jets of air to fly. An octopus uses jets of water to dart through the sea.

Tentacle tales

A Norwegian story tells of the Kraken, a sea monster that wrapped its giant arms around ships and sank them. The legend may be based on the mysterious giant squid that live in deep waters.

Funnel

Long arms to grasp prey

Flexible funnel

At the edge of the octopus's baglike body is a funnel. It can bend to aim the jet of water backward or forward.

Powerful suckers grip the rock so octopus can pull itself along

1 On the bottom

The common octopus hides during the day in its rocky lair, coming out at night to look for food, such as crustaceans.

Sucker is sensitive to touch and taste

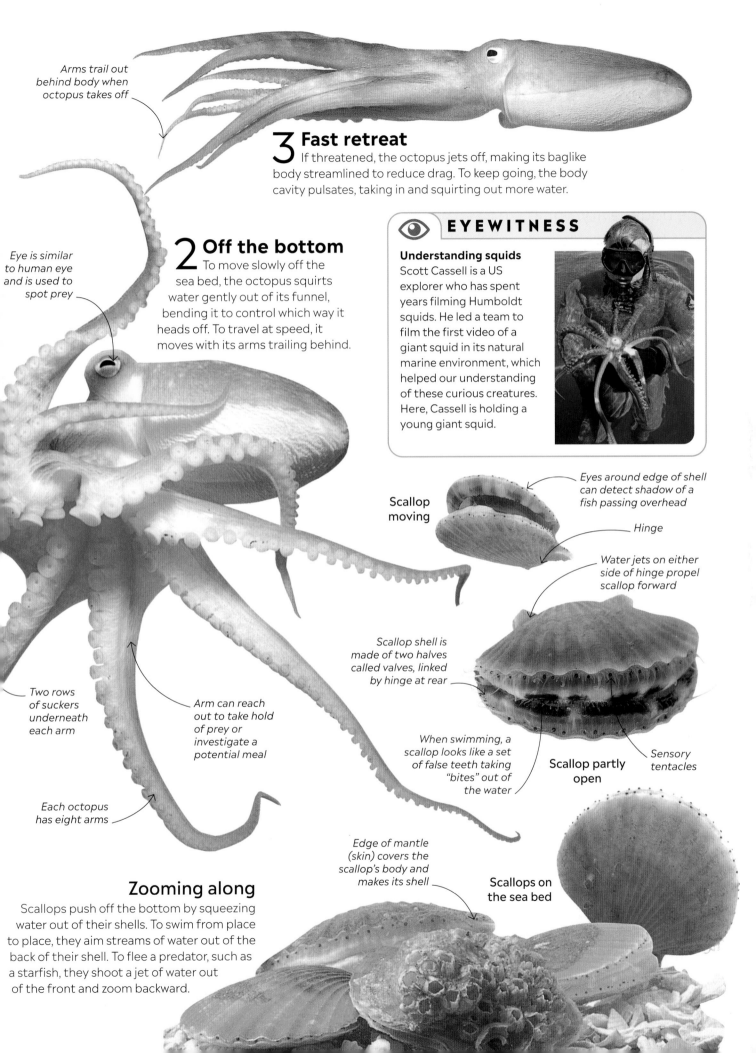

Arms trail out behind body when octopus takes off

3 Fast retreat

If threatened, the octopus jets off, making its baglike body streamlined to reduce drag. To keep going, the body cavity pulsates, taking in and squirting out more water.

2 Off the bottom

To move slowly off the sea bed, the octopus squirts water gently out of its funnel, bending it to control which way it heads off. To travel at speed, it moves with its arms trailing behind.

Eye is similar to human eye and is used to spot prey

👁 EYEWITNESS

Understanding squids
Scott Cassell is a US explorer who has spent years filming Humboldt squids. He led a team to film the first video of a giant squid in its natural marine environment, which helped our understanding of these curious creatures. Here, Cassell is holding a young giant squid.

Eyes around edge of shell can detect shadow of a fish passing overhead

Scallop moving

Hinge

Water jets on either side of hinge propel scallop forward

Scallop shell is made of two halves called valves, linked by hinge at rear

When swimming, a scallop looks like a set of false teeth taking "bites" out of the water

Scallop partly open

Sensory tentacles

Two rows of suckers underneath each arm

Arm can reach out to take hold of prey or investigate a potential meal

Each octopus has eight arms

Edge of mantle (skin) covers the scallop's body and makes its shell

Scallops on the sea bed

Zooming along

Scallops push off the bottom by squeezing water out of their shells. To swim from place to place, they aim streams of water out of the back of their shell. To flee a predator, such as a starfish, they shoot a jet of water out of the front and zoom backward.

Moving along

Seawater is denser than air, making it harder to move through. To be a fast swimmer, it helps to have a shape that is streamlined like a torpedo to reduce drag (resistance to water). The density of seawater helps support an animal's body weight. Some ocean animals get up enough speed underwater to leap briefly into the air, but not all are good swimmers. Many can only swim slowly, drift in the currents, crawl along the bottom, or burrow in the sand. Others simply stay put, anchored to the sea bed.

The **blue whale** is the heaviest animal, weighing up to **165 tons (150 tonnes).**

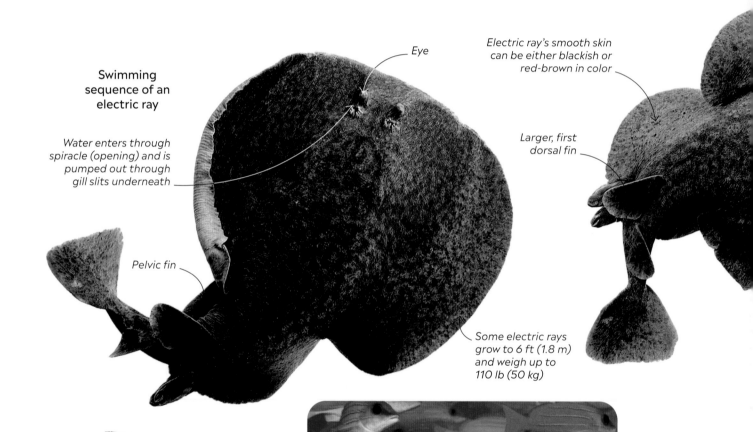

Swimming sequence of an electric ray

Water enters through spiracle (opening) and is pumped out through gill slits underneath

Eye

Electric ray's smooth skin can be either blackish or red-brown in color

Larger, first dorsal fin

Pelvic fin

Some electric rays grow to 6 ft (1.8 m) and weigh up to 110 lb (50 kg)

Flying fish

To escape predators, flying fish can gather speed, leap into the air, and spread their side fins to glide for more than 30 seconds.

At school

Fish often swim together in a shoal or a school (like these blue-striped snappers). The moving mass of fish makes it harder for a predator to target one individual and there are more pairs of eyes to detect danger.

Diving deep

True seals use front flippers to steer and move by beating their back flippers from side to side. Harbor seals (left) can dive to 300 ft (90 m) and hold their breath for 28 minutes, but elephant seals dive to more than 4,900 ft (1,500 m) and can stay underwater for two hours. When underwater, seals close their nostrils to stop water from entering the airways and use oxygen stored in the blood and muscles.

Bottlenose dolphins reach speeds of up to 17 mph (27 kph)

Out of the water

Dolphins leap out of water to signal to other dolphins, when feeding, and for fun. They also porpoise (skim over water for short distances) when moving at speed, which saves energy.

Pectoral fin provides extra propulsion as waves pass along flexible edges of its rounded side

Smaller, second dorsal fin

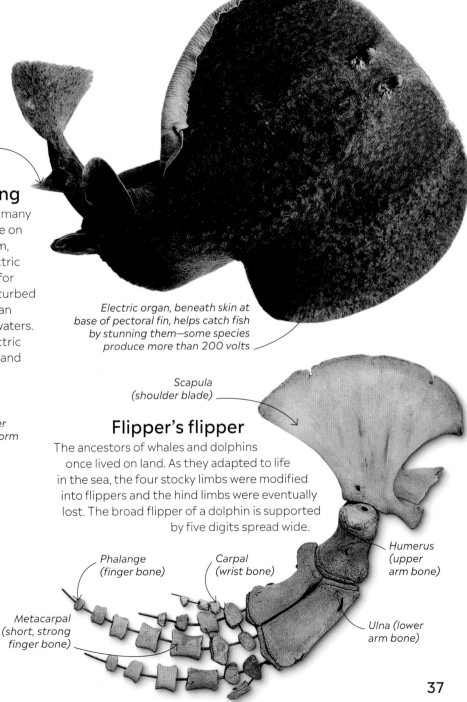

In the swing

During the day, many electric rays hide on the sandy bottom, relying on their electric organs and camouflage for defense, but they swim if disturbed and at night in search of prey. There are more than 50 species of electric ray, mostly living in warm waters. Most other rays have spindly tails (unlike the electric ray's broad tail, used like a shark's for swimming) and move through water using their pectoral fins.

Electric organ, beneath skin at base of pectoral fin, helps catch fish by stunning them—some species produce more than 200 volts

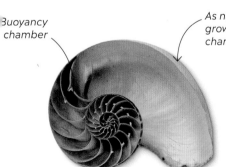

Buoyancy chamber

As nautilus grows, larger chambers form

Afloat

The gas-filled sections of the chambered nautilus's shell help keep it afloat. The nautilus itself lives in the last and biggest chamber and moves by jet propulsion (pp.34–35).

Scapula (shoulder blade)

Flipper's flipper

The ancestors of whales and dolphins once lived on land. As they adapted to life in the sea, the four stocky limbs were modified into flippers and the hind limbs were eventually lost. The broad flipper of a dolphin is supported by five digits spread wide.

Phalange (finger bone)

Carpal (wrist bone)

Humerus (upper arm bone)

Metacarpal (short, strong finger bone)

Ulna (lower arm bone)

Stalked barnacles on driftwood

Ocean
travelers

Some sea animals travel great distances to find places to feed and breed. Whales feed in the cold, food-rich waters of the far north or south, then travel to warm, tropical waters to breed. Turtles, seals, and seabirds feed out at sea but come ashore to reproduce. Seals come ashore to digest their meal. Salmon grow in the ocean and return to rivers to breed. Ocean currents help speed animals on their way. Even animals that cannot swim can hitch a ride on another animal or drift on a piece of wood.

Barnacles adrift

Barnacles grow on rocks, ships' hulls, and even turtles and whales. These goose barnacles can drift long distances on pieces of wood. Barnacles are crustaceans (like crabs and lobsters) and have shell-like plates that protect their bodies.

Larger eyes form when adult eel migrates to sea

Skin turns silver before eel migrates back to Sargasso Sea

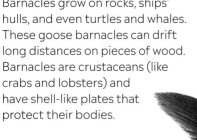

Leaflike larva (young), called Leptocephalus

Young eel, known as elver or glass eel

Portuguese man-of-war

Not a true jellyfish but a siphonophore (made up of a colony of special polyps), the man-of-war has a gas-filled float that keeps it at the surface, where it is blown by the wind and drifts with the currents

Trailing tentacles armed with stings that can kill small fish

Mysterious journey

For centuries, no one knew where European eels went to breed—only that young eels came back to rivers in large numbers. Then scientists found the smallest larvae were in the Sargasso Sea in the western Atlantic where the adults breed. The larvae are carried by ocean currents to Europe and turn into elvers.

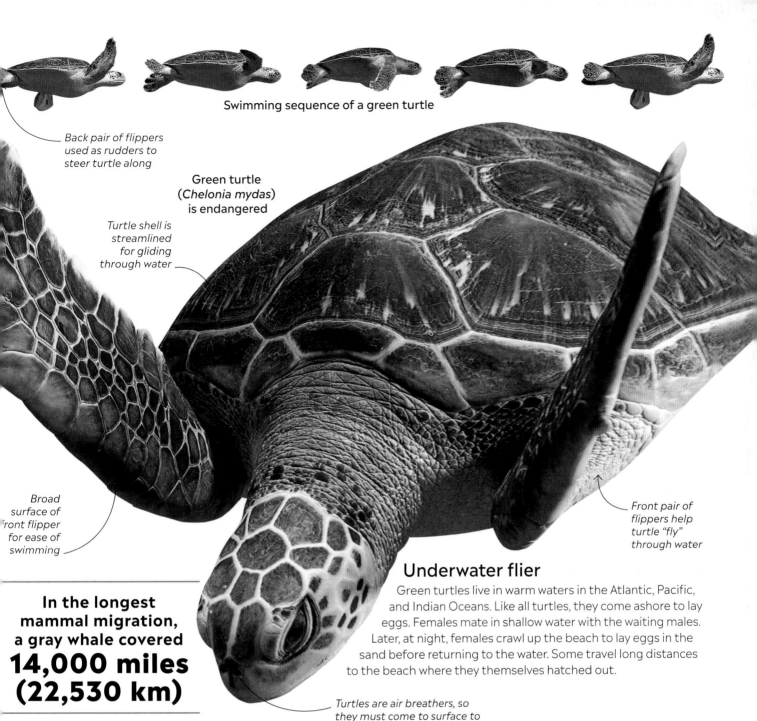

Swimming sequence of a green turtle

Back pair of flippers used as rudders to steer turtle along

Green turtle (*Chelonia mydas*) is endangered

Turtle shell is streamlined for gliding through water

Broad surface of front flipper for ease of swimming

Front pair of flippers help turtle "fly" through water

Underwater flier

Green turtles live in warm waters in the Atlantic, Pacific, and Indian Oceans. Like all turtles, they come ashore to lay eggs. Females mate in shallow water with the waiting males. Later, at night, females crawl up the beach to lay eggs in the sand before returning to the water. Some travel long distances to the beach where they themselves hatched out.

In the longest mammal migration, a gray whale covered 14,000 miles (22,530 km)

Turtles are air breathers, so they must come to surface to breathe through their nostrils

Electronic tagging

James Ketchum Mejía studies migratory marine species and is an authority on hammerhead sharks' movements. He attaches electronic sensors, called tags, to ocean animals to track them, understand how they migrate, and learn what habitats they prefer. This helps in conservation efforts.

Turtle trip

In Japanese legend, Urashima Taro rides into the sea on a turtle. After some time, he yearns for home. The sea goddess gives him a box that he must never open. Back home, he finds everything has changed and no one knows him. He opens the box and breaks the spell, turning into a very old man because he has spent 300 years at sea.

The twilight zone

Around 660–3,300 ft (200–1,000 m) below the surface is the twilight zone. Fish living here often have rows of light organs on their bellies to help camouflage them against the little light that filters down from above. Many animals shelter in the twilight zone by day, hiding from daytime hunters such as seabirds. They swim upward to feed in the food-rich surface water at night. Others spend most of their lives in the zone, eating any available food.

Hunter of the depths
Viper fish have an impressive set of long, daggerlike teeth to grab fish prey, which they attract with a lure dangling from the front of the dorsal fin. To swallow prey, such as a hatchet fish (see right), the hinged jaws open very wide.

Glass jellies
Glass jellyfish live in every ocean, from the sunlit upper zone to depths of 2,300 ft (700 m). They have a deep bell and a long mouth, which twists around to catch tiny prey. They can also display beautiful rainbow colors.

A giant of a squid
The Atlantic giant squid can weigh as much as 1.1 tons (1 tonne). Suckers on the tentacles cling onto prey, and sperm whales often bear the scars of an attack.

Jumbo squid can reach 12 ft (3.6 m) from head to tentacle tip

Mythical merman
Strange creatures lurk in the depths, but nothing like this.

Sail-like dorsal fin can be raised and lowered

Long and skinny
The lancet fish has a narrow body, lightweight bones, and little muscle. It catches squid and other fish living at the same depths.

Lancet fish can grow nearly 6½ ft (2 m) long

Extremely tiny second dorsal fin is fleshy

Lancet fish swims below the warm surface waters of the Atlantic, Pacific, and Caribbean

Model of a lancet fish

Deep scattering layer

World War II sonar operators mapping the sea floor recorded readings of an echo they thought was the sea floor, but during the night, it seemed to rise. The echo was due to a mass migration of millions of sea creatures such as plankton, jellyfish, shrimp, small fish, and squid reflecting the sonar when they swam upward to feed. Today, it is known as the "deep scattering layer."

Sonar operator during World War II

Model of a hatchet fish, *Sternoptyx*

Sharply angled dorsal fin

Silvery body helps camouflage fish in right light

Deep-sea hatchet

Hatchet fish have silvery, bladelike bodies. The light organs along their belly and tail, when viewed from below, are just bright enough to help them blend in with the sunlit water above. Hatchet fish live in the Atlantic, Pacific, and Indian Oceans.

Light organs located on belly

Large first dorsal fin

Upward-pointing eye helps locate prey

Symmetrical tail fin

Dorsal fin can be used for herding fish prey

Model of a hatchet fish, *Opisthoproctus*

Tube along belly produces light to avoid being spotted from below

Looking up

This is another type of hatchet fish. It has large, tubular eyes pointing upward so it can detect the faintest glimmer of light produced by potential prey. This fish is found in oceans around the world below regions with warm surface waters.

Large gill flap

Colors (instead of light organs) help fish blend into light ocean above and dark ocean below

Pelvic fin

Pectoral fin

Pointed teeth for grabbing fish

The darkest depths

There is no light in the oceans below 3,300 ft (1,000 m)—just blackness. Many fish in the dark zone are black, too, and almost invisible. Light organs are used as signals to find a mate or to lure prey. Food is scarce in the cold depths. Small organisms eat tiny food fragments that rain from above as "marine snow." They are prey for larger animals, including squids and slow-swimming fish with huge mouths and stretchy stomachs.

Lateral line organs sense vibrations in water made by moving prey

Umbrella mouth gulper

The gulper eel swims along slowly with its huge mouth wide open, ready to swallow any food it finds, such as shrimp and small fish. The adults live in the lower part of the twilight zone and in the dark zone. The leaflike larvae are found in the sunlit zone from 330–660 ft (100–200 m). As they grow, the young gulper eels descend into deeper water.

Gulper eel lives in the dark depths below temperate and tropical surface waters

Tiny eye on end of nose

Long lower jaw

Adults grow to about 30 in (75 cm) from the tip of their long tail to the head

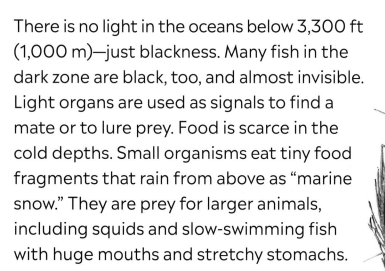

Invisible fish

Scientists studying deep-water fish such as the common fangtooth (above) have found that they hide in open water by being black. This deep color is possible because of tiny structures in the skin that absorb light rather than reflecting it, which would have made them visible to predators or prey.

Fishing line

The whipnose has a long, whiplike lure for attracting passing prey. The prey approaches, mistaking the lure for food, and is then snapped up.

Model of a whipnose, which lives in the Atlantic and Pacific Oceans

Whipnose grows to 5 in (13 cm) length

Binocular eyes

Gigantura's extraordinary tubular eyes are probably used to pinpoint the glowing light organs of its prey. Its skin can stretch so that it can swallow fish larger than itself.

Lower lobe of tail fin is longer than upper lobe

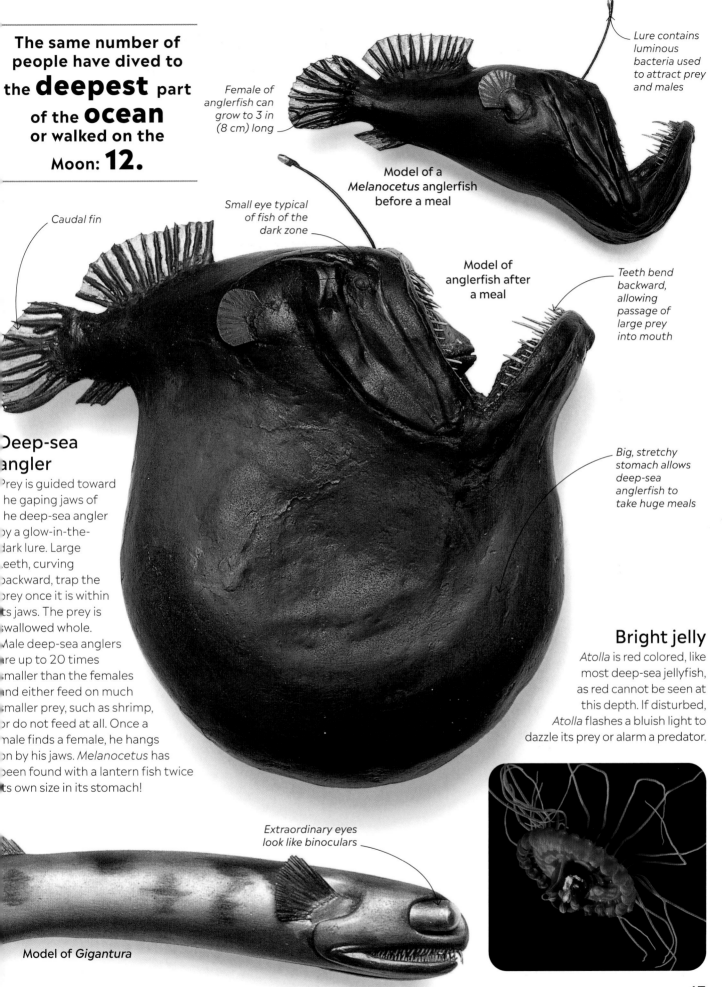

Caudal fin

Small eye typical of fish of the dark zone

Female of anglerfish can grow to 3 in (8 cm) long

Model of a *Melanocetus* anglerfish before a meal

Lure contains luminous bacteria used to attract prey and males

Model of anglerfish after a meal

Teeth bend backward, allowing passage of large prey into mouth

Deep-sea angler

Prey is guided toward the gaping jaws of the deep-sea angler by a glow-in-the-dark lure. Large teeth, curving backward, trap the prey once it is within its jaws. The prey is swallowed whole. Male deep-sea anglers are up to 20 times smaller than the females and either feed on much smaller prey, such as shrimp, or do not feed at all. Once a male finds a female, he hangs on by his jaws. *Melanocetus* has been found with a lantern fish twice its own size in its stomach!

Big, stretchy stomach allows deep-sea anglerfish to take huge meals

Bright jelly

Atolla is red colored, like most deep-sea jellyfish, as red cannot be seen at this depth. If disturbed, *Atolla* flashes a bluish light to dazzle its prey or alarm a predator.

Extraordinary eyes look like binoculars

Model of *Gigantura*

43

On the bottom

The bottom of the deep ocean has little food, and it is dark and cold. Much of the sea bed is covered with soft clays or mudlike oozes made of skeletons of tiny sea animals and plants. Some animals feed on the sea bed, extracting small food particles from the ooze. Others filter nutrients from the water. These tiny food particles are the remains of dead animals (and their droppings) and plants that have sunk down from above. Because food is scarce and temperatures are so low, most animals living in the deep ocean take a long time to grow.

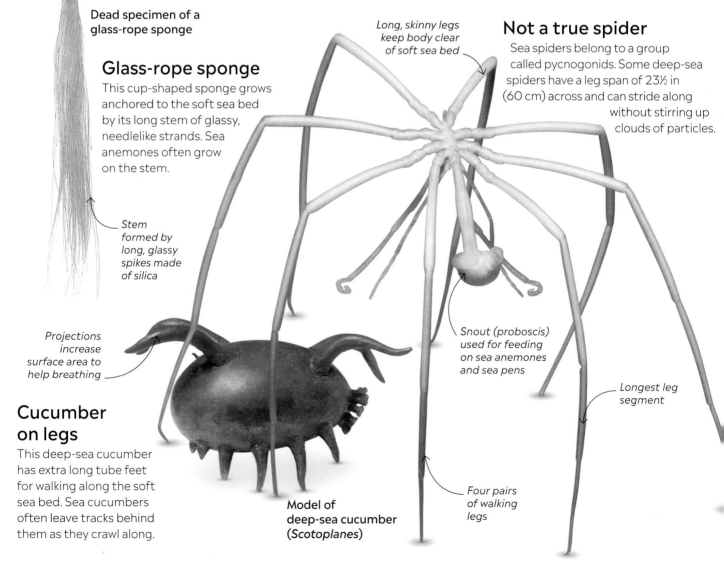

Dried remains of sea anemones

Dead specimen of a glass-rope sponge

Glass-rope sponge

This cup-shaped sponge grows anchored to the soft sea bed by its long stem of glassy, needlelike strands. Sea anemones often grow on the stem.

Stem formed by long, glassy spikes made of silica

Long, skinny legs keep body clear of soft sea bed

Not a true spider

Sea spiders belong to a group called pycnogonids. Some deep-sea spiders have a leg span of 23½ in (60 cm) across and can stride along without stirring up clouds of particles.

Projections increase surface area to help breathing

Cucumber on legs

This deep-sea cucumber has extra long tube feet for walking along the soft sea bed. Sea cucumbers often leave tracks behind them as they crawl along.

Model of deep-sea cucumber (*Scotoplanes*)

Snout (proboscis) used for feeding on sea anemones and sea pens

Longest leg segment

Four pairs of walking legs

Lily of the deep

Sea lilies use feathery arms to gather food particles from the water. Many live in trenches that are 330–26,000 ft (100–8,000 m) deep. Some are anchored to the sea bed. Those with whorls of spikes (cirri) around their stems can move by using their arms, dragging the stems behind.

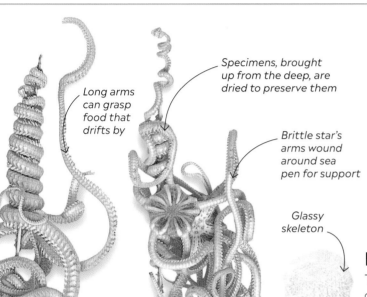

Long arms can grasp food that drifts by

Specimens, brought up from the deep, are dried to preserve them

Brittle star's arms wound around sea pen for support

Glassy skeleton

Stem of sea pen grows up from the sea bed

STARTING ON THE BOTTOM

Often mistaken as tidal waves, tsunamis are caused by earthquakes or eruptions on the sea bed sending shock waves through the water. The waves race across the open sea. When they near the coast, they bunch up into towering walls of destruction.

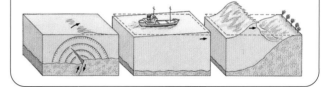

Flower baskets

The glassy skeletons of Venus flower basket sponges are admired for their beauty, but the living sponge is covered with soft tissues. Most glass sponges live in deep waters, but some live in shallower waters in cold, polar regions.

Dried Venus flower basket (*Euplectella aspergillium*)

Opening of sponge covered with sieve plate

Dried deep-sea brittle stars (*Asteronyx loveni*)

All in the arms

Deep-sea brittle stars use long, snakelike arms to cling onto sea pens and to feed on small creatures and other food particles drifting by. Climbing off the sea bed gives them a good chance of collecting food. Brittle stars are common bottom dwellers at any depth, but these deep-sea ones live at 330–5,900 ft (100–1,800 m).

Deep heat

In parts of the ocean floor, very hot, mineral-rich water gushes out. These vents, or hot springs, exist where the plates that make up Earth's crust are moving apart. Cold seawater sinks deep into cracks, where it is heated. At temperatures of up to 752°F (400°C), hot water spews out, carrying minerals that form chimneys (black smokers). These allow life to exist without sunlight. Special bacteria harvest energy from the minerals and create food from the hydrogen sulfide in the water. These bacteria support the animals found only on vents.

GROWING OCEAN

New areas of ocean floor are created at spreading centers between two tectonic plates. When hot, molten rock (lava) spills from the crust, the lava cools and hardens, adding material to the edge of both plates. Old areas of ocean floor are destroyed when one plate slides under another.

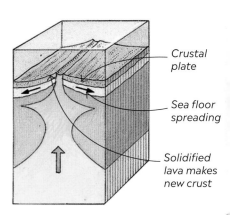

Crustal plate

Sea floor spreading

Solidified lava makes new crust

Black smoker
Animal life abounds in an active vent site, such as this one in the Mid-Atlantic Ridge. If a vent stops producing hot, sulfur-rich water, the community is doomed unless it can find a new site.

Model of hydrothermal vents found in the eastern Pacific

Plumes of hot water are rich in sulfides, which are poisonous to most animals

Dense numbers of animals crowd around a vent

Tube wor can gr to 10 (3 m) lor

Giant clams in the eastern Pacific can grow to 12 in (30 cm) long

Some animals graze on mats of bacteria covering rocks near a vent

Chimney made from mineral deposits as hot vent water mixes with cold seawater

Black smoker chimney can reach 33 ft (10 m) high

Pioneering submersible
The US submersible *Alvin* was the first to take scientists down to observe marine life near the Galápagos vents in the eastern Pacific in the 1970s. Since then, *Alvin* has made many dives to vents around the world to depths of 12,500 ft (3,800 m).

Vent communities

Vent communities vary. This model shows black smokers in the eastern Pacific, where giant clams and tube worms are the most distinctive animals—as are hairy snails in the Mariana Trench and eyeless shrimp along the Mid-Atlantic Ridge.

Giant tube worm has bacteria inside its body, which provide it with food

Fish predators nibble tops off tube worms

Underwater diver

This diver, wearing a wetsuit with an aqualung, gets air through a line from the tank on the back. The wetsuit prevents the diver from becoming too cold, helping them stay in the water longer.

Diverse divers

People have always wanted to explore the sea to find wrecks and treasure, study marine life, and drill for oil and gas. The first diving kit was a simple bell with air. Later, diving suits with hard helmets helped divers go deeper and stay longer, with air pumped down a line. In the 1940s, the aqualung or SCUBA (Self-Contained Underwater Breathing Apparatus) enabled divers to carry a tank with air on their back.

Life saver

The weight of water increases pressure on the body. If a diver comes up too quickly after a long or deep dive, the sudden drop in pressure can cause the nitrogen in the air supply to form bubbles in the blood and tissues. This is called decompression sickness (the bends). A decompression chamber raises the pressure to move the bubbles out through the lungs, then slowly lowers it to the normal level at the surface.

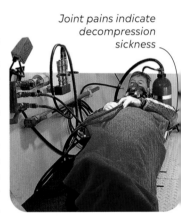

Joint pains indicate decompression sickness

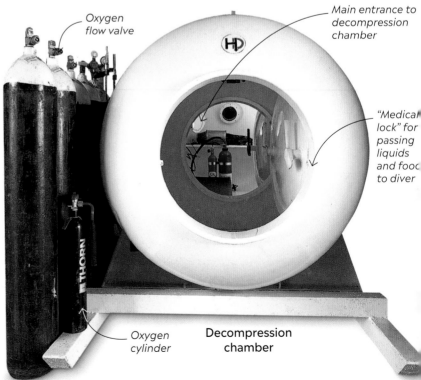

Oxygen flow valve

Main entrance to decompression chamber

"Medical lock" for passing liquids and food to diver

Oxygen cylinder

Decompression chamber

Rope connecting bell to surface

Wooden bell

Weight

Helmet equipped with two-way communication system so diver can talk to someone on the surface

Helmet made of copper and brass

Face plate

Breastplate screwed to tunic using six, eight, or twelve bolts

Wrench for tightening bolts on breastplate

Early diving bell

In 1690, Edmund Halley's diving bell allowed divers to be resupplied with barrels of air that were lowered from the surface and linked to the bell and divers by a tube. The bell was used at depths of 60 ft (18 m).

Long johns made from wool for greater warmth and insulation

A classic diving suit

The "Standard" diving suit was invented by Augustus Siebe in the 1830s. Modified versions of this hard-helmeted suit are still in use today. The tunic made of layers of canvas and rubber is waterproof. The copper and brass helmet fits onto a heavy breastplate (corselet), which is bolted onto the tunic. Wearing heavy boots and two extra weights, the diver would sink to depths of about 200 ft (60 m).

Rubber cuff for extra waterproofing

Suit made of a layer of rubber between two layers of canvas

Ribbed cuff helps trap warm air

Diver has two weights—one at the front, a second at the back

Weight is about 30 lb (13 kg)

Complete "Standard" diving suit

Leather boot with lead base to help weigh down diver in water

Each boot weighs 18 lb (8 kg)

An early diving suit

Submarines

The first submarines were simple designs that could travel a short distance underwater and were useful in warfare. Later versions were powered by diesel or gasoline while on the surface and by batteries underwater. Since 1955, nuclear power has allowed submarines to travel great distances before refueling. Today, they use sonar and computer systems to navigate, track other vessels, and launch missiles.

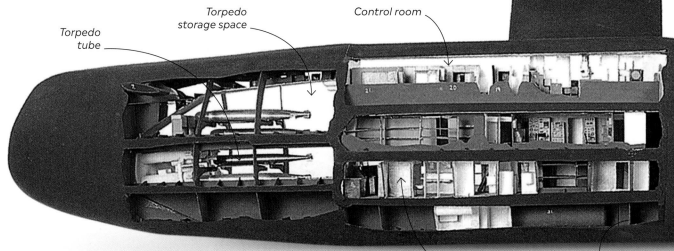

Tower with snort mast, periscope, and radar aerials

Torpedo tube

Torpedo storage space

Control room

Living quarters

Ballast tank takes in water to submerge

Model of HMS _Dreadnought_

Auger drills into enemy ship to attach mine

Snort mast renews and expels air with help of bellows

Delayed action mine

Vertical propeller

Side propeller powered by foot pedals

"Turtle" hero

A one-man wooden submarine, the _Turtle_, was used during the Revolutionary War in 1776 to try to attach a mine to an English ship that was blockading New York Harbor. The effort was not a success.

Underwater adventure

Inspired by the invention of modern submarines, this 1900 engraving shows a scene in the year 2000 with people enjoying a submarine journey. Tourists can take trips in small submarines to view marine life in the Red Sea and the Caribbean. However, most people explore the ocean by learning to SCUBA dive or snorkel.

Inside story

The cramped interior of a submersible has only just enough room for a pilot and possibly one or two passengers.

Driving console

👁 **EYEWITNESS**

Deep diver
Former NASA astronaut Kathryn Sullivan traveled in the submersible *Limiting Factor* to become the first woman to reach the deepest point in the ocean, Challenger Deep. Undersea explorer Victor Vescovo went with her.

Whale-shaped

HMS *Dreadnought* had a single propeller at its tail end. It also had a snort mast, while a whale has a blow-hole on the top of its head. A whale must surface for air, but HMS *Dreadnought* could spend weeks submerged. Operating from 1960 to 1981, it had an 88-person crew and was Britain's first nuclear-powered submarine.

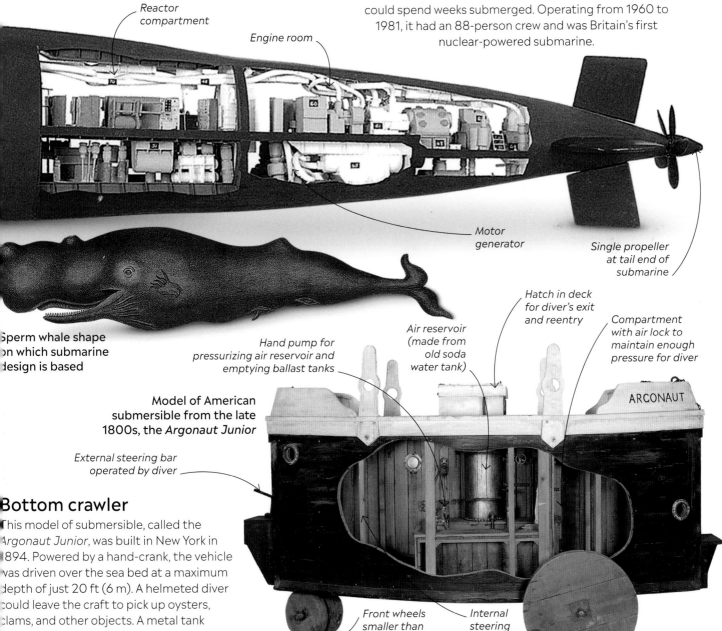

Reactor compartment

Engine room

Motor generator

Single propeller at tail end of submarine

Sperm whale shape on which submarine design is based

Model of American submersible from the late 1800s, the *Argonaut Junior*

Hand pump for pressurizing air reservoir and emptying ballast tanks

Air reservoir (made from old soda water tank)

Hatch in deck for diver's exit and reentry

Compartment with air lock to maintain enough pressure for diver

ARCONAUT

External steering bar operated by diver

Bottom crawler

This model of submersible, called the *Argonaut Junior*, was built in New York in 1894. Powered by a hand-crank, the vehicle was driven over the sea bed at a maximum depth of just 20 ft (6 m). A helmeted diver could leave the craft to pick up oysters, clams, and other objects. A metal tank contained the diver's air supply and a garden hose linked the tank to the helmet.

Front wheels smaller than back ones for easier turning

Internal steering position

51

Ocean explorers

The ocean has always been a place of mystery. The first depth soundings were made by dropping a lead weight on a line until it hit the bottom. Echo sounders, invented during World War I, bounced pulses of sound off the sea bed. This led to sonar systems that could map the ocean floor. For centuries, the only clues to deep-sea life were creatures brought up in fishermen's nets or washed ashore. Today, submersibles reach otherwise inaccessible waters, but much of the ocean is yet to be explored.

Microscope used by a marine biologist in Scotland during the late 1800s

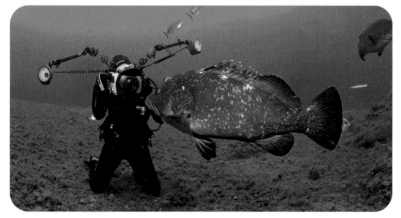

SCUBA diving

SCUBA equipment has proved invaluable in the study of marine life in shallow waters. Instead of bringing animals into an aquarium, marine biologists can observe them in the wild.

GLORIA AT WORK

To survey the sea bed, GLORIA was towed behind its mother ship at a speed of 10 knots. Sound pulses would span across the sea bed for up to 18 miles (30 km) on each side. It picked up echoes from features on the sea bed, which were used to produce maps of the sea floor.

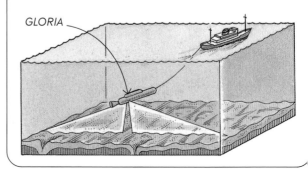

GLORIA

Deep stars

Many submersibles have been used for underwater exploration. The deepest dive ever was to 35,800 ft (10,912 m) in the Mariana Trench in 1960.

Deep Star *can reach depth of 4,000 ft (1,200 m)*

Mechanical arm used to lower Autosub into the water

Autosub

This Autonomous Underwater Vehicle (AUV) can explore remote parts of the ocean. AUVs are unmanned and operate without being tethered to a ship or submersible.

Autosub uses a suite of sensors to collect data

Research vessel

Modern research vessels carry sophisticated equipment for studying the ocean. This vessel, National Oceanic Atmospheric Administration (NOAA)'s *Oscar Dyson*, has six laboratories along with computers and monitoring devices to study fish populations. It also has sound-reducing machines so scientists can study the fish without disturbing them.

Glorious GLORIA

Geological Long Range Inclined Asdic (sonar), or GLORIA, surveyed the ocean floor. Covering 7,700 sq miles (20,000 sq km) in a day, it scanned more than 5 percent of the world's oceans in 20 years.

Cable drum

GLORIA was towed by the nose

Rope guide, used during recovery of GLORIA

Inside GLORIA are two rows of transducers, which emit sounds (sonar pulses)

Torpedo-shaped body (towfish) is 26 ft (8 m) long and weighs about 2.2 tons (2 tonnes)

Launching cradle weighs about 14.3 tons (13 tonnes)

Cable 1,300 ft (400 m) long contains electrical wiring for signaling

Cradle's hydraulic system tipped GLORIA into the water

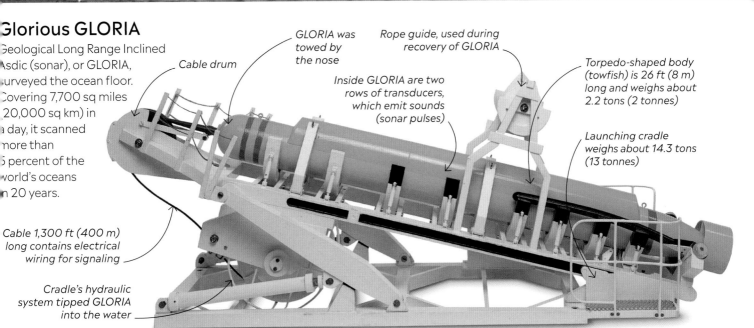

Wrecks on the sea bed

Ever since people took to the sea in vessels to travel and trade between countries, there have been wrecks on the sea bed. Mud and sand cover wooden hulls, protecting the timbers by keeping out the oxygen, which speeds up decay. Metal-hulled ships are badly corroded by water; the *Titanic*'s hull could disintegrate in a few decades. Wrecks in shallow water get covered by plant and animal life, turning them into living reefs. Uncovering wrecks and their objects can tell us much about life in the past.

Valuable property
In 1892, divers worked on the wreck of the tug *L'Abeille* off Le Havre, France, to bring up (salvage) items of value.

Sad reminders
Many items recovered from the *Titanic* wreck were not valuable, but everyday items such as this cutlery remind us of those who used them before they died.

The unsinkable ship
In 1912, the *Titanic* sailed from England to New York on her first voyage. When she hit an iceberg, she took 2 hours and 40 minutes to sink, with only 705 people saved out of 2,228. The wreck was found in 1985 by a French-US team using remote-controlled video equipment on an uncrewed probe.

Plane wreck
This "flying boat" seaplane crashed into the water off the coast of West Papua, Indonesia. The Bermuda Triangle in the Atlantic is famous for the many planes that mysteriously vanished there.

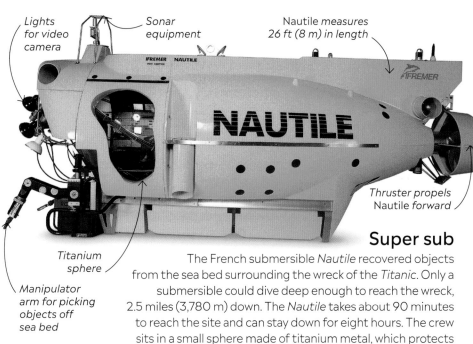

Lights for video camera

Sonar equipment

Nautile measures 26 ft (8 m) in length

Thruster propels Nautile forward

Titanium sphere

Manipulator arm for picking objects off sea bed

Super sub

The French submersible *Nautile* recovered objects from the sea bed surrounding the wreck of the *Titanic*. Only a submersible could dive deep enough to reach the wreck, 2.5 miles (3,780 m) down. The *Nautile* takes about 90 minutes to reach the site and can stay down for eight hours. The crew sits in a small sphere made of titanium metal, which protects them from the huge pressure at these depths.

The United Nations estimates that the number of shipwrecks on Earth's ocean floors is
higher than 3 million.

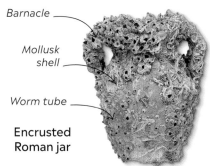

Barnacle

Mollusk shell

Worm tube

Encrusted Roman jar

Sea bed home

Barnacle shells and worm tubes grew on this Roman jar for hundreds of years on the sea bed. Archaeologists try to raise and clean such objects without damaging them.

Glittering gold

Spanish coins, much in demand by pirates, sometimes ended up on the sea bed when a ship sank.

Less valuable silver coin

 EYEWITNESS

Salcombe treasure

In 1995, divers of the South West Maritime Archaeology Group found treasure—jewelry and gold ingots and coins—from a 17th-century shipwreck at the Salcombe Cannon site in the UK. This is the largest-ever find of Moroccan gold in Europe, some of which is shown here with one of the divers who found it.

55

Harvesting fish

More than 99 million tons (90 million tonnes) of fish are caught around the world each year. Some fish are caught by hand-thrown nets and traps in local waters, but far more are caught at sea by fishing vessels using the latest technology. Some fish are caught on long lines with many hooks or ensnared when they swim into long walls of drift nets more than 1 mile (1.5 km) in length. If too many fish are caught, then stocks take a long time to recover. In many countries, fish is the main source of protein.

There are about
4 million fishing
vessels in the
world's oceans.

At sea
Atlantic salmon spend up to four years at sea, feeding on other fishes and putting on tens of pounds annually. Then the mature salmon return to the home rivers and streams where they hatched. They recognize their home stream by a number of clues, including the water's "smell." Farmed salmon are usually much smaller.

Large first dorsal fin

Fin rays are well developed

Pelvic fin

Pectoral fin

Operculum (flap covering gills)

Teeth for gripping slippery prey

Fish farming
To meet the demand for fish, some species such as bass, sea bream, and salmon are reared in sea cages in fish farms, but fish farms can cause problems, too. Young salmon are reared in freshwater and then released into pens in calm seawaters. Uneaten food and fish waste in the sea around fish farms can damage the marine environment.

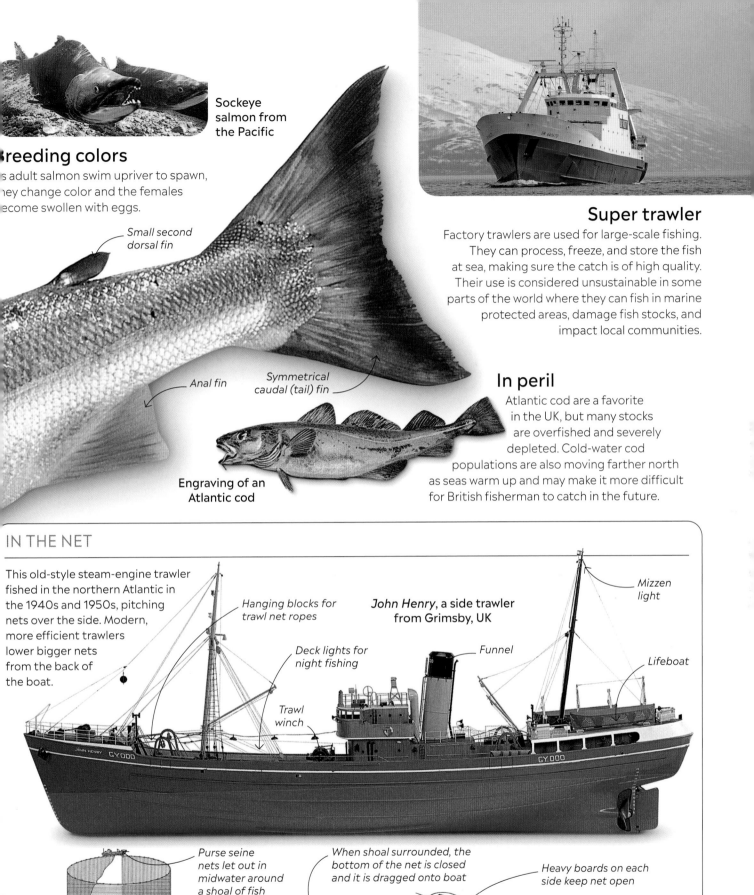

Sockeye salmon from the Pacific

Breeding colors

As adult salmon swim upriver to spawn, they change color and the females become swollen with eggs.

Small second dorsal fin

Anal fin

Symmetrical caudal (tail) fin

Engraving of an Atlantic cod

Super trawler

Factory trawlers are used for large-scale fishing. They can process, freeze, and store the fish at sea, making sure the catch is of high quality. Their use is considered unsustainable in some parts of the world where they can fish in marine protected areas, damage fish stocks, and impact local communities.

In peril

Atlantic cod are a favorite in the UK, but many stocks are overfished and severely depleted. Cold-water cod populations are also moving farther north as seas warm up and may make it more difficult for British fisherman to catch in the future.

IN THE NET

This old-style steam-engine trawler fished in the northern Atlantic in the 1940s and 1950s, pitching nets over the side. Modern, more efficient trawlers lower bigger nets from the back of the boat.

Hanging blocks for trawl net ropes

Deck lights for night fishing

Trawl winch

John Henry, **a side trawler from Grimsby, UK**

Funnel

Mizzen light

Lifeboat

Purse seine nets let out in midwater around a shoal of fish

When shoal surrounded, the bottom of the net is closed and it is dragged onto boat

Heavy boards on each side keep net open

Trawl net

Weights at bottom and floats at top of net help keep it straight

Purse seine nets

Bottom trawls sweep along sea bed

Fish are caught in end of net

Ocean products

People have always harvested plants and animals from the ocean, from fish, mollusks (clams, squid), and crustaceans (shrimp, lobsters) to sea cucumbers and seaweeds. Most are collected for food, although some animals and seaweeds are now cultivated to meet demand for products and to avoid overcollecting the ocean's wildlife. Some sea creatures are made into amazing products, many of which (such as mother-of-pearl buttons) are now replaced by synthetic materials.

Yarn dyed purple from pigment of sea snails

Royal purple
Sea snails were used to make a purple dye for clothes worn by kings in ancient times. The liquid was extracted from huge quantities of salted snails left in vats gouged out of rocks, then heated to concentrate the dye.

Seaweed farm
Seaweed is farmed and used as food and medicine. In Japan, seaweeds are used in crackers and to wrap raw fish parcels (sushi). The most important is a kelp called wakame. Seaweed is grown on bamboo poles, collected, and dried. The red seaweed's jellylike agar is used in foods and medical research. Seaweeds are also used as fertilizers and may be used as a biofuel to replace liquid fossil fuels in the future (see p.60).

Soft skeleton
Bath sponges grow among sea grasses in reef lagoons. When brought up from the sandy sea bed, the sponges are covered with slimy, living tissues. Natural sponges are prone to diseases and overcollecting.

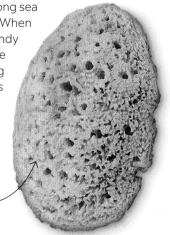

Soft skeleton left after processing living sponge

EYEWITNESS

Medicinal sponges
Scientists at the Institute of Chemistry of Nice (ICN), France, are studying substances found in some marine animals, such as sponges, that could help treat human diseases. They are developing new testing methods for these chemicals and enzymes, which may be used in medicines for cancer and Alzheimer's. A diver collects sea sponges here.

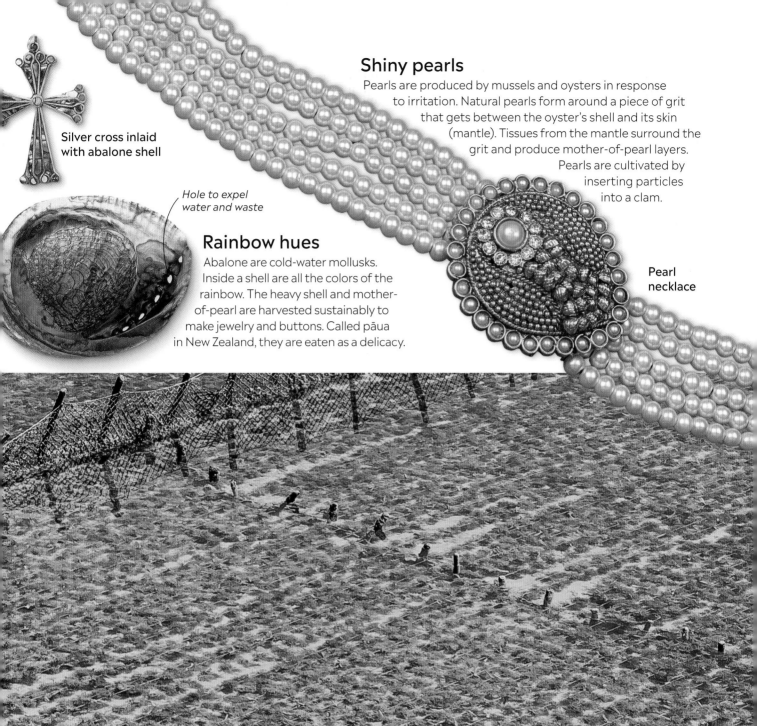

Silver cross inlaid with abalone shell

Shiny pearls

Pearls are produced by mussels and oysters in response to irritation. Natural pearls form around a piece of grit that gets between the oyster's shell and its skin (mantle). Tissues from the mantle surround the grit and produce mother-of-pearl layers. Pearls are cultivated by inserting particles into a clam.

Hole to expel water and waste

Rainbow hues

Abalone are cold-water mollusks. Inside a shell are all the colors of the rainbow. The heavy shell and mother-of-pearl are harvested sustainably to make jewelry and buttons. Called pāua in New Zealand, they are eaten as a delicacy.

Pearl necklace

Golden threads

n the Mediterranean, he pen shell produces a hick mat of silky byssus hreads. These threads vere once collected; pun into fine, golden hread; and then woven nto cloth. Perhaps this loth started the Ancient Greek legend of the olden fleece.

Gloves can be made from byssus threads of noble pen shell

Tapered shell is brittle

Byssus threads made by shell to anchor it to sea bed

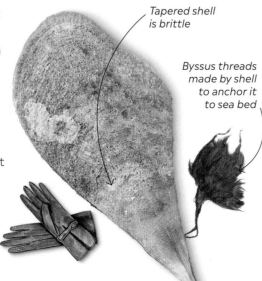

Salt harvesting

When seawater evaporates, a salt-crystal crust is left behind. Large quantities of sea salt are produced by flooding shallow ponds (salterns) with seawater and letting the water evaporate in the hot Sun. Sea salt is still produced in places with warm weather and little rain.

Energy from the ocean

Our industrial world is powered largely by oil and gas, and valuable reservoirs of oil and gas lie hidden beneath the sea bed on the continental shelf. When oil and gas are discovered, permanent oil platforms, firmly anchored to the sea bed, drill for oil, which is piped ashore or stored on floating vessels (FPSOs). However, there is a growing concern that fossil fuels are a major cause of climate change, causing a threat to life in the sea and on land, including humans (see p.62). Developments in technology can harness the power from waves, ocean currents, wind, and even sunlight.

On fire
Oil and gas are highly flammable. Accidents such as the North Sea's Piper Alpha disaster in 1988, when 167 people died, have led to improved safety measures.

DEATH AND DECAY

Plant and animal remains fell to the ancient sea bed and were covered by layers of mud. Heat and pressure turned them into oil, then gas, which rises.

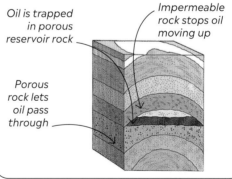

Oil is trapped in porous reservoir rock

Impermeable rock stops oil moving up

Porous rock lets oil pass through

Tallest structure on this platform is flare stack for safety reasons

Fireproof lifeboat gives better chance of survival

Floating production
Floating vessels called FPSOs (Floating Production, Storage, Offloading) store the oil and gas produced from nearby drilling platforms and undersea wells until it is taken away by tankers. FPSOs work well in deepwater locations that are too far to connect to the shore by sea-bed pipelines. They can also move out of the way of hurricanes or drifting icebergs.

Wind turbines
Oil reservoirs run dry, but wind turbines are a source of renewable energy. As the wind blows the sails of these turbines, they generate electricity. This is the North Hoyle Offshore Wind Farm in Wales, UK.

Newt suit

A thick-walled suit resists pressure. When underwater, the diver breathes air at normal pressure as if inside a submersible. This allows a diver to go deeper without having to undergo decompression (see p.48). Newt suits (right) are used in oil exploration to depths of 1,200 ft (365 m).

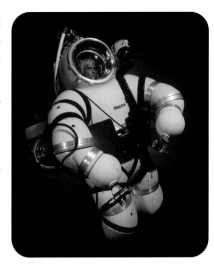

Tide mill

In the past, windmills powered by the wind, and water mills powered by rivers and tides, were used to grind corn. Tide mills use water trapped from the rising tide, which is then released to power the mill.

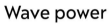

Wave power

Waves, ocean currents, and tidal flow can be harnessed to produce energy. Turbines and wind energy converters create electricity from the moving ocean, which is transported to the shore by special power cables. Wave energy may also be harnessed to help power scientific equipment on the sea bed that currently runs on batteries.

👁 EYEWITNESS

Deborah Greaves
An ocean engineer, Deborah Greaves is an authority on marine renewable energy. She has helped develop new types of wave energy converters and worked on projects aimed to set up large-scale wave energy farms all over Europe. Greaves also gives talks on renewable energy sources, as shown here.

Oceans in **peril**

Oceans and ocean life are under threat. Overharvesting has depleted many ocean animals, from whales to fishes, while sewage and industrial waste are dumped into the sea, carrying chemicals that disrupt the food chain. Oil spills smother and poison marine life. Nets and trash dumped at sea can choke turtles or trap birds. Today, laws help stop ocean pollution and protect marine life, but global warming remains a serious threat to it.

Jewelry made of teeth of great white shark, now vulnerable

Oil spill

Oil is needed for industry and motor vehicles and to make plastic. Huge quantities are brought up from the sea bed, transported in tankers, and sent along pipelines. Accidents happen where massive amounts of oil are spilled. Oil-soaked seabirds and sea mammals die of cold, because their feathers or fur no longer contain pockets of air to keep them warm.

Cleaning up the ocean
Global Ghost Gear Initiative is a group of many organizations and individuals working to rid oceans of "ghost gear"—lost or discarded fishing equipment. Environmentalists, such as the ones shown here, try to remove large fishing nets floating or on the sea bed, as these continue to trap marine creatures.

Climate change

Burning fossil fuels, such as oil, coal, and natural gas, increases greenhouse gases in the atmosphere. This leads to a rise in air and water temperatures, causing glaciers and ice in polar regions to melt. Animals, such as polar bears, rely on sea ice to survive. With sea ice slowly disappearing, they are losing their habitat and are under threat.

Worse for whales

For centuries, whales have been hunted for their meat, oil, and bones. Whale oil was used in foods, as lubricants, and in soap and candles, and the broad baleen plates were made into household items. Commercial whaling drastically reduced whale numbers. Most kinds of whales are now protected, but some are still caught for food. They are also in danger due to climate change and a rise in pollution.

Japanese painting showing early whalers in pursuit of whales

Saving beauty

This chambered nautilus shell was carved in the 17th century. The six kinds of nautilus in the Pacific and Indian Oceans are at risk from overcollecting. They are hunted at night when they rise to the surface. Chambered nautili grow very slowly, reaching maturity in six or more years, so populations can take a long time to recover.

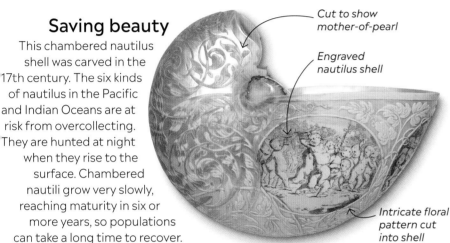

Cut to show mother-of-pearl

Engraved nautilus shell

Intricate floral pattern cut into shell

Take care

Sea life is fragile. A basket sponge this size may be 100 years old, but it could be damaged by a diver's kick. All kinds of junk on the sea bed is smothering marine life. In the 1997–1998 El Niño, sea temperatures rose by 2–4°F (1–2°C) in parts of the Indian Ocean, causing some corals to eject their algae partners and die. Many scientists think global warming may have contributed to the unusual temperature rise.

Oceans absorb 30 percent of the carbon dioxide that human activity adds to the atmosphere, causing a rise in **carbonic acid** in the oceans.

Did you **know?**

AMAZING FACTS

The world's oceans contain 97 percent of Earth's water. Of the remaining 3 percent, just over 2 percent is locked in ice and just under 1 percent is fresh water.

The Pacific Ocean, at 59 million sq miles (153 million sq km), covers about one-third of Earth's surface.

Pacific Ocean as seen from space

The coldest sea surface is in the White Sea, in the Arctic, at 28.4°F (−2°C). The warmest is in summer in shallow parts of the Indian Ocean's Persian Gulf, at 96.1°F (35.6°C).

The temperature of the oceans' deepest water is between 34–39°F (2–4°C).

The highest mountain underwater is in the Pacific Ocean, near New Zealand. At 5.4 miles (8.7 km) tall, it is nearly as high as Mount Everest—Earth's highest mountain.

The greatest tidal range and the highest tides in the world occur in Canada's Bay of Fundy, in the Atlantic, where the difference between low and high tides can be up to 52 ft (16 m).

Of all marine life, 90 percent occurs in the sunlit, or euphotic, zone—the surface layer of the ocean where there is enough light to support photosynthesis. Here, plankton provide the basis of the ocean's food chain.

A bucket of seawater can contain up to 10 million phytoplankton and zooplankton. Most phytoplankton are less than 0.0003 in (0.01 mm) wide.

The largest meat-eating fish is the great white shark. Some grow up to 20 ft (6 m) long and weigh around 1.65 tons (1.5 tonnes).

A great white shark can detect one part of blood from a wounded animal in 100 million parts of water.

Tiny cleaner wrasse at work inside the mouth of a grouper fish

Small fish called cleaner wrasse feed on parasites that infest much larger fish, such as a grouper, even swimming right inside the larger fish's mouth to feed.

To flee predators, flying fish can leap 6 ft (2 m) out of the water and "fly" 325 ft (100 m) on outspread fins.

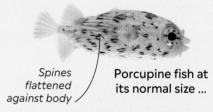

Spines flattened against body

Porcupine fish at its normal size ...

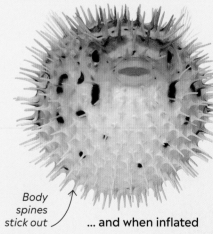

Body spines stick out

... and when inflated

If threatened, a porcupine fish takes in water to swell its body to twice its normal size, making it too large and uncomfortable to swallow.

At birth, a blue whale can weigh about 3.3 tons (3 tonnes). The babies guzzle 22½ gallons (100 liters) of their mother's milk a day and grow at almost 11 lb (5 kg) an hour.

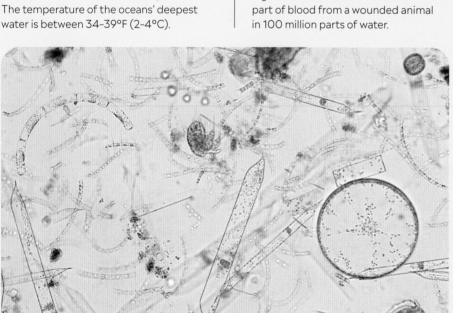

Plankton magnified several hundred times

QUESTIONS AND ANSWERS

Why is the sea salty?

Salt is washed out of Earth's rock, sand, and soils by rainwater, then carried in streams and rivers to the sea. Over millions of years, this has built up the sea's concentration of salt.

What causes waves?

Most waves are created by the wind blowing across the ocean. Their height depends on the strength and duration of the wind.

Waves forming out at sea

Why is the sea blue?

The water acts like a filter. Sunlight is made up of many colors. Red light is absorbed by the sea and the remaining blue light is scattered by the water and reflected to the surface. This makes the sea look blue.

How many types of fish are there?

There are around 25,000 species of marine and freshwater fish. Around 24,000 are bony fishes; 1,100 are cartilaginous or gristly fishes; and about 100 are jawless fishes.

Larger upper tail vane

Tail vanes equal in size

Cartilaginous fish—blacktip reef shark (top); and bony fish—mackerel (above)

How do cartilaginous and bony fish differ?

Bony fish have bony skeletons, while sharks and rays have skeletons made of cartilage (gristle). Bony fish also have a gas-filled swim bladder to control buoyancy, so they remain still. Gristly fish will start to sink if they don't keep moving. Bony fish have tail vanes of equal size and protective gill flaps, whereas most sharks have larger upper tail vanes than lower ones and gill slits without flaps.

How do fish hide from predators in the open sea?

Fish that live near the surface have dark backs and paler bellies that help camouflage them from above and below. Fish on the sea bed can blend in with their surroundings.

Stargazer hiding in gravel on the sea bed

RECORD BREAKERS

- **Largest sea creature**
  The blue whale is the world's largest animal, at up to 98 ft (30 m) long and as much as 165 tons (150 tonnes) in weight.

- **Biggest fish**
  The whale shark can grow up to 41.5 ft (12.65 m) and weigh 22 tons (20 tonnes).

- **Smallest fish**
  The adult Marshall Islands dwarf goby is just 0.3 in (6 mm) from nose to tail.

- **Fastest fish**
  The sailfish can reach speeds of up to 68 mph (109 kph)—faster than a cheetah can run.

- **Heaviest bony fish**
  The ocean sunfish, or *Mola mola*, can weigh up to 2.2 tons (2 tonnes).

Whale shark

The world's oceans

There are five ocean basins that connect to form one global ocean. These include the Pacific, Atlantic, Indian, and Arctic Oceans, which fill natural basins in Earth's crust. The Southern Ocean is technically part of the southern Pacific, Atlantic, and Indian Oceans but is officially delimited from them south of 60 degrees latitude.

PACIFIC OCEAN

The Pacific Ocean is the world's largest ocean, covering 28 percent of Earth's surface. It has 20,000–30,000 islands and is surrounded by a "Ring of Fire," where tectonic activity causes frequent eruptions and quakes.

AREA: 58,957,258 sq miles (152,617,160 sq km)

Includes: Bali Sea, Bering Sea, Bering Strait, Coral Sea, East China Sea, Flores Sea, Gulf of Alaska, Gulf of Tonkin, Java Sea, Philippine Sea, Savu Sea, Sea of Japan, Sea of Okhotsk, South China Sea, Tasman Sea, Timor Sea

AVERAGE DEPTH: 13,874 ft (4,229 m)

Unmanned submersible Kaiko reached the bottom of Mariana Trench in 1995

DEEPEST POINT: 36,201 ft (11,034 m) Challenger Deep in the Mariana Trench

COASTLINE: 84,299 miles (135,663 km)

CLIMATE: Strong currents and trade winds constantly blow across the Pacific's waters, often causing violent tropical storms.

NATURAL RESOURCES: Fish stocks, oil and gas fields, sand and gravel aggregates.

ENVIRONMENTAL ISSUES: Nearly half of the world's shipping routes cross the Pacific, including huge supertankers, bulk carriers, and container ships. As a result, the ocean suffers from oil pollution, which threatens marine life and seabirds. Some of the

Pacific's endangered marine creatures include dugongs, sea otters, sea lions, seals, turtles, and whales.

Coral atoll reef in the southwest Pacific

ATLANTIC OCEAN

The Atlantic is the world's second-largest ocean, covering about one-fifth of Earth's surface. An underwater mountain chain called the Mid-Atlantic Ridge runs down its center.

AREA: 31,477,905 sq miles (81,527,400 sq km)

Includes: Baltic Sea, Black Sea, Caribbean Sea, Davis Strait, Denmark Strait, Gulf of Guinea, Gulf of Mexico, Labrador Sea, Mediterranean Sea, North Sea, Norwegian Sea, Sargasso Sea, Scotia Sea

AVERAGE DEPTH: 12,391 ft (3,777 m)

DEEPEST POINT: 28,232 ft (8,605 m) Milwaukee Deep in the Puerto Rico Trench

COASTLINES: 69,512 miles (111,866 km)

CLIMATE: Northerly waters are usually covered with sea ice in winter. The Gulf Stream—a warm water current—flows from the Gulf of Mexico, north and then east, which raises the temperatures of northern Europe and keeps many northern ports ice-free during the winter.

Panama Canal links Atlantic and Pacific

NATURAL RESOURCES: Fish, oil, gas, sand, gravel.

ENVIRONMENTAL ISSUES: Some Atlantic waters are polluted by industrial waste, sewage, and oil. Fish stocks have run low because of overfishing, especially with trawling for bottom-living fish, such as cod.

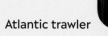

Atlantic trawler

INDIAN OCEAN

The Indian Ocean is the world's third-largest ocean. Its northern currents flow southwest along the coast of Somalia in winter and in the opposite direction in summer.

Endangered green turtle

AREA: 26,050,133 sq miles (67,469,536 sq km)

Includes: Andaman Sea, Arabian Sea, Bay of Bengal, Great Australian Bight, Gulf of Aden, Gulf of Oman, Java Sea, Mozambique Channel, Persian Gulf, Red Sea, Strait of Malacca, Timor Sea

AVERAGE DEPTH: 12,720 ft (3,877 m)

DEEPEST POINT: 23,376 ft (7,125 m) Java Trench, also called Sunda Trench

COASTLINE: 41,338 miles (66,526 km)

CLIMATE: Cool, dry winds blow from the northeast in February and March. In August and September, southwesterly winds bring monsoon rain and flooding.

NATURAL RESOURCES: Oil and gas fields, sand and gravel, fish.

ENVIRONMENTAL ISSUES: Oil pollution; endangered sea life includes the dugong, turtles, and whales.

Oil production in the Arabian Sea

ARCTIC OCEAN

The Arctic Ocean is the world's smallest ocean. Between December and May, most of the ocean is covered by polar ice.

AREA: 3,350,023 sq miles (8,676,520 sq km)

Includes: Baffin Bay, Barents Sea, Beaufort Sea, Chukchi Sea, East Siberian Sea, Greenland Sea, Hudson Bay, Kara Sea, Laptev Sea, Northwest Passage

AVERAGE DEPTH: 6,349 ft (1,935 m)

DEEPEST POINT: 18,635 ft (5,680 m) Fram Basin

COASTLINE: 28,203 miles (45,389 km)

Steel-hulled ice breakers crush ice and open up a lane for other ships

CLIMATE: Polar, with continuous cold and narrow annual temperature ranges.

NATURAL RESOURCES: Oil and gas, sand and gravel, fish, marine mammals.

ENVIRONMENTAL ISSUES: Loss of sea ice due to climate change, which is threatening the polar bear's habitat.

Polar bear

Partly webbed front paws for swimming

SOUTHERN OCEAN

The Southern Ocean is the world's fourth-largest ocean. Parts of the ocean freeze in winter, forming the vast Ronne and Ross ice shelves.

AREA: 8,097,843 sq miles (20,973,318 sq km)

Includes: Amundsen, Bellingshausen, Ross, and Weddell Seas

AVERAGE DEPTH: 14,760 ft (4,500 m)

DEEPEST POINT: 23,737 ft (7,235 m) South Sandwich Trench

COASTLINE: 11,165 miles (17,968 km)

CLIMATE: Polar, with continuous cold and narrow annual temperature ranges.

NATURAL RESOURCES: Probable large oil and gas fields, sand, gravel, fish, krill.

ENVIRONMENTAL ISSUES: Ultraviolet radiation penetrating through the ozone hole above the Antarctic is damaging phytoplankton. Despite treaties, illegal and unregulated fishing still occurs, but protected whale and fur seal populations are making a comeback after overhunting in the 18th and 19th centuries.

Characteristic flat-topped Antarctic iceberg

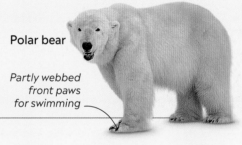

Statistics compiled from data from the Naval Oceanographic Office, Stennis Space Center, Mississippi (2001)

Find out more

There is a wealth of information available about the oceans and marine life. If you do not live (or go on vacation) near the sea, your first stop should be an aquarium. Look out, also, for excellent wildlife programs on television, or search the Internet using the websites listed below as a starting point.

Razor shell encrusted with barnacle, oyster (behind), and slipper limpet

Sea shells

If you visit the beach, look out for sea shells washed up on the shore. Bring a guidebook to help you identify them. Always put inhabited shells back where you find them, and never collect shells from a protected site. Removing shells can damage the ecosystem.

Visit an aquarium

Plan a visit to an aquarium to observe a huge range of marine life from all over the world. Many aquariums have impressive viewing tanks containing hundreds of species from jellyfish and octopuses to sharks and starfish. Look out for special events where you can get up close to sharks, rays, and other marine creatures.

USEFUL WEBSITES

- News and information on the oceans:
  www.nationalgeographic.com/environment/topic/oceans
- Homepage of the Monterey Bay Aquarium, with live web cams:
  www.montereybayaquarium.org
- National Marine Sanctuaries:
  www.sanctuaries.noaa.gov
- Find out what you can do to help the ocean:
  www.mcsuk.org
- Marine Life Information Network:
  www.marlin.ac.uk

Study a rock pool

Rock pools are fascinating microhabitats filled with a wide variety of plants and animals. Even if you visit the same one several times, it is unlikely you will find the same creatures. Look out for starfish; anemones; mussels; and seaweed, such as sea lettuce and kelp. If you stay still, you may spot crabs hiding in crevices between rocks, or a tiny fish.

Face to face

You can see marine life up close if you take a trip in a glass-bottomed boat or a tourist submarine. Or try snorkeling—it's amazing what you can see once you're below the ocean's surface, especially if you snorkel over a coral reef.

S.E.A. AQUARIUM, SINGAPORE

Has more than 100,000 marine animals from over 800 species and includes:
· The huge Open Ocean tank with 50,000 marine animals
· Home to the world's largest collection of manta rays in an aquarium setting

GEORGIA AQUARIUM, ATLANTA, GEORGIA

Biggest aquarium in the US. It features:
· Displays of beluga whales, whale sharks, and sea lions
· A discovery zone with marine adventures for visitors

THE DEEP, HULL, UK

Includes more than 100 species of marine fish and features:
· One of the deepest display tanks in Europe, descending 33 ft (10 m) and including several species of shark
· Displays of marine life in different environments, from coral lagoons to the twilight zones and the polar oceans

MARY ROSE MARITIME MUSEUM, PORTSMOUTH, UK

The Tudor flagship's museum, with:
· Exhibits on the ship's salvage and restoration
· Displays of artifacts and crew's personal possessions

Pewter jug from the *Mary Rose*

Flukes (tail parts) of a humpback whale

Whale watching

Various companies organize whale-watching tours, giving you the chance of seeing whales in their natural environment. The tourists pictured left are observing humpback whales off the coast of Alaska.

Marine sanctuaries

Marine sanctuaries are established to protect local wildlife and educate the public about the marine environment. Why not plan a trip to a sanctuary or find out more about them through the Internet? You can also join organizations working to protect and conserve the world's oceans.

Otter in the Monterey Bay National Marine Sanctuary, off the coast of California

Glossary

Bioluminescence

ABYSSAL PLAIN
The flat floor of an ocean basin covered in a layer of sediment. (*see also* BASIN, SEDIMENT)

ANTARCTIC
Region at the South Pole, south of the Antarctic Circle.

ARCTIC
Region at the North Pole, north of the Arctic Circle.

ATOLL
Coral reef surrounding a lagoon, growing on the rim of a volcanic island that has sunk.

BASIN
Large, natural bowl-shaped indentation in Earth's crust. Four of the world's oceans lie in such basins.

BIOLUMINESCENCE
Meaning living (bio) light (luminescence)—the production of light by a living organism. Some deep-sea creatures produce their own light. In others, it is produced by bacteria living in them.

BIVALVE
Soft-bodied animal living in a hinged shell, such as a clam or an oyster.

BLACK SMOKER
Tall, chimneylike vent on the ocean floor that belches out super-hot water containing chemicals used by some deep-sea creatures to make food. Black smokers occur at volcanically active spots on mid-ocean ridges. (*see also* MID-OCEAN RIDGE)

BONY FISH
Fish such as mackerel or cod with a bony skeleton and a swim bladder to control buoyancy.

CARTILAGINOUS FISH
Fish such as a shark or ray, with a gristly or cartilaginous skeleton and no swim bladder, meaning it will sink if it does not keep moving.

CEPHALOPOD
Type of mollusk with a soft body and suckered tentacles, such as a squid or octopus.

CONTINENTAL CRUST
The parts of Earth's crust that form the planet's continents.

CONTINENTAL DRIFT
Theory that Earth's continents were once a single mass of land that slowly drifted apart over millions of years and are still moving today.

CONTINENTAL SHELF
Sloping submerged land at a continent's edge.

Krill

CONTINENTAL SLOPE
Sloping submerged land that descends from the continental shelf to the abyssal plain, forming the side of an ocean basin. (*see also* ABYSSAL PLAIN, BASIN)

COPEPOD
Tiny, shrimplike creature, forming part of the ocean's zooplankton. (*see also* ZOOPLANKTON)

CRUSTACEAN
Animal, such as a crab or krill, with jointed legs and a tough, jointed outer skeleton over its body.

CURRENT
Body of water that flows through the sea; there are both surface and deep-water currents.

DARK ZONE
Area of the ocean bordered by the twilight zone above and the abyss below, from around 3,300–13,200 ft (1,000–4,000 m) deep. Also called the bathypelagic zone.

DIATOM
Single-celled alga and type of phytoplankton that floats near the ocean's surface, forming the basis of an ocean food chain or food web; common in cool waters.

DORSAL FIN
Fin on the back of a fish that helps it keep its balance as it swims.

ECHINODERM
Marine invertebrate with spines in the skin, such as a starfish.

EL NIÑO
Warm-water current that flows east toward the western coast of South America every few years, causing weather changes all over the world.

FOOD CHAIN
Series or group of plants and animals linked by their feeding relationships. A food chain usually includes algae or plants, plant-eating animals, and meat-eating animals.

FOOD WEB
A series of several interlinked food chains.

HURRICANE
Tropical storm with winds of more than 74 mph (119 kph), forming over the Atlantic Ocean. Tropical storms are usually called typhoons in the Pacific Ocean and cyclones in the Indian Ocean.

Swirling winds of a hurricane forming over the Atlantic

Starfish (an echinoderm)

ICEBERG
Floating mass of ice broken off an ice sheet or glacier, carried along by ocean currents.

INVERTEBRATE
Animal without a backbone.

KRILL
Shrimplike crustacean that lives in Arctic and Antarctic waters in great numbers, forming much of the food supply of baleen whales.

MAGMA
Molten rock that lies beneath Earth's crust.

MARINE BIOLOGY
The study of ocean life.

MID-OCEAN RIDGE
Long, undersea mountain range forming where two tectonic plates are pulling apart, with magma rising from beneath Earth's surface and hardening into rock.

MOLLUSK
An invertebrate with a soft body, usually enclosed by a shell. Includes bivalves (such as clams), gastropods (such as sea slugs), and cephalopods (such as squid and octopuses). (see also BIVALVE, CEPHALOPOD)

OCEANOGRAPHY
The scientific study of the oceans.

PHYTOPLANKTON
Microscopic single-celled algae that drift in the ocean's sunlit zone. (see also SUNLIT ZONE)

PLANKTON
Tiny plant and animal organisms that drift in surface waters and are the basis of most marine food chains. (see also FOOD CHAIN, ZOOPLANKTON)

PLATE TECTONICS
The study of the movement of the lithospheric plates that carry oceanic and continental crusts.

POLYP
A sea anemone or coral with a mouth surrounded by tentacles. A hard coral polyp makes a limestone cup, or skeleton, to protect its body. Thousands of polyps live together in colonies, forming a coral reef.

ROV
Short for Remotely Operated Vehicle—a small vessel operated from (and tethered to) a submersible or ship.

SALINITY
Amount of dissolved salt in seawater. Salinity is measured as parts of salt per 1,000 parts of seawater; the average salinity of the oceans is 35 parts of salt per 1,000 parts of seawater.

SCUBA
Stands for Self-Contained Underwater Breathing Apparatus—SCUBA divers carry their own air supply in tanks on their backs.

SEA
Another word for ocean, or a particular part of an ocean—for example, the Black Sea and the Mediterranean Sea are connected to the Atlantic Ocean.

SEAMOUNT
Underwater volcano that rises 3,280 ft (1,000 m) or more above the surrounding plain.

SEDIMENT
Mud, sand, and silt, containing millions of tiny plants and animals, washed off the land by rivers. Sediment settles on the ocean floor.

SONAR
Short for Sound Navigation And Ranging—a system that can locate the position of an object by emitting sounds, then timing the echoes that bounce back.

SUBMERSIBLE
Manned or remotely operated underwater research submarine designed to withstand water pressure in the deep water. (see also WATER PRESSURE)

SUNLIT ZONE
Surface layer of ocean penetrated by sunlight, to around 660 ft (200 m) deep. Most marine life lives here. Also called the epipelagic zone.

SYMBIOSIS
Close interaction between two different species where either, both, or neither benefit from the relationship.

Black smoker

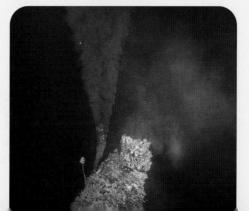

TIDE
The regular rise and fall of the sea caused by the gravitational pull of the Sun and the Moon on our planet.

TRENCH
A steep-sided trough or valley in the ocean floor.

TSUNAMI
Sea wave usually caused by an underwater volcanic eruption or earthquake. It can cause great damage if it reaches the coast, as it may gain considerable height in shallow water. Sometimes wrongly called a tidal wave, a tsunami has no connection to the tide.

TWILIGHT ZONE
Area of the ocean from around 660–3,300 ft (200–1,000 m) deep, bordered by the sunlit zone above and darkness below. Also called the mesopelagic zone.

TYPHOON
Name given to a tropical storm in the western Pacific Ocean. (see also HURRICANE)

UPWELLING
Rising of cool, nutrient-rich water from deeper parts of the ocean to the surface, where phytoplankton and other marine life gather to feed. (see also PHYTOPLANKTON)

Submersible

WATER PRESSURE
Force exerted by water because of its weight and density; water pressure increases by one atmosphere for each 33 ft (10 m) depth.

WAVE HEIGHT
The distance between the crest (top of a wave) and its trough (lowest part of a wave).

WAVELENGTH
The vertical distance between two successive wave crests (the tops of the waves).

ZOOPLANKTON
Tiny animals that float in the water, such as copepods and tiny crustaceans, forming part of plankton. (see also PHYTOPLANKTON, PLANKTON)

Index

Acknowledgments

The publisher would like to thank the following people for their help with making the book: For their invaluable assistance during photography – The University Marine Biological Station, Scotland, especially Prof. John Davenport, David Murden, Bobbie Wilkie, Donald Patrick, Phil Lonsdale, Ken Cameron, Dr. Jason Hall-Spencer, Jason Thurston, Steve Parker, Geordie Campbell, and Helen Thirlwall; Sea Life Centres (UK), especially Robin James, David Copp, Patrick van der Menve, and Ian Shaw (Weymouth); and Marcus Goodsir (Portsmouth); Colin Pelton, Peter Hunter, Dr. Brian Bett, and Mike Conquer of the Institute of Oceanographic Sciences;Tim Parmenter, Simon Caslaw, and Paul Ruddock of the Natural History Museum, London; Margaret Bidmead of the Royal Navy Submarine Museum, Gosport; IFREMER for their kind permission to photograph the model of *Nautile*; David Fowler of Deep Sea Adventure; Mak Graham, Andrew and Richard Pierson of Otterferry Salmon Ltd; Bob Donalson of Angus Modelmakers; Sally Rose for additional research; Kathy Lockley for providing props; Helena Spiteri, Djinn von Noorden, Susan St. Louis, Ivan Finnegan, Joe Hoyle, Mark Haygarth, and David Pickering for editorial and design assistance; Neville Graham, Sue Nicholson, and Susan St. Louis for the wallchart; Trevor Day for his assistance on the paperback edition; Saloni Talwar and Priyanka Sharma-Saddi for the jacket; Vagisha Pushp for picture research; Ann Baggaley for proofreading; and Helen Iddles for the index.

The publisher would like to thank the following for their kind permission to reproduce their images:
(Key: a=above, b=bottom, c=centre, f=far, l=left, m=middle, r=right, t=top)

Alamy Images: blickwinkel / Hecker 37tl, blickwinkel / R. Koenig 25tl, Cultura Creative Ltd / Zac Macaulay 48l, John Gaffen 61br,
Paul Glendell 60-61c, Gon2Foto / Richard Mittleman 29tc, Jane Gould 36bc, Renato Granieri 62-63b, imageBROKER / Norbert Probst 22-23t, imageBROKER / SeaTops 30tl, markferguson2 61crb, Matthew Oldfield Underwater Photography 54-55c, Minden Pictures / Mark Carwardine 35cra, Minden Pictures / Pete Oxford 39bc, Mochet / Andia 57tr, Nature and Science 51tr, Nature Photographers Ltd / Paul R. Sterry 10cr, Nature Picture Library / Solvin Zankl 40tr, PA Images 60clb, PA Images / By Ben Curtis 55br, Pally 18b, 42clb, Panther Media GmbH / Uebama 61ca, Pictorial Press Ltd 7tr, Jeff Rotman 63tr, Science History Images / Photo Researchers 12clb, Stephen Frink Collection 25cb, Steve Bloom Images 37tr, Underwater Imaging 31tr, United Archives GmbH / IFTN 54bl, WaterFrame_fur 64tr, Wildestanimal 29tl; **Dorling Kindersley:** Oxford Museum of Natural History / Gary Ombler 6bc, University Marine Biological Station, Millport, Scotland / Frank Greenaway 4tl, Jerry Young 2tr; **Dreamstime.com:** Almir1968 45cra, Antos777 1c, Conchasdiver 22bc, Paul Hampton 34c; **Heather Angel:** 38bc; **Ardea**/Val Taylor: 63c; **Bridgeman Art Library**/Prado, Madrid 8tr; **Bruce Coleman Ltd:** Carl Roessler 22br, Jane Burton 38bl; **Corbis:** Ralph White 67c, 71bc, Roger Wood 67tr, Tom Stewart 66br; **Mary Evans Picture Library:** 19tl, 33tr, 34tr, 40cb, 45tr, 49tl, 49bl, 50br, 54c; **Getty Images:** AFP / Jiji Press 17c, AFP / Pius Utomi Ekpei 60bl, Fairfax Media Archives / Simon Alekna 15ca, Image Source 68cra, Los Angeles Times / Allen J. Schaben 21tc, Moment / Brett Monroe Garner 67cla, Moment / Douglas Klug 10-11c, Paris Match Archive / Jean-Louis Atlan 9cra, Popperfoto 41cla, Science Photo Library / Choksawatdikorn 64bl, Science Photo Library / Mark Garlick 12-13t, The Image Bank Unreleased / Audrey Gibson 68bl, The Image Bank Unreleased / Xu Xiaolin 51tl, Universal History Archive / Universal Images Group 2bl, 43tr; Nikolas Konstatinou 69tl; **Getty Images / iStock:** E+ / elmvilla 67b, E+ / NNehring 26tr, Placebo365 62cra, sserg_dibrova 22bl, Kaitlin Viera 28tr;

Robert Harding Picture Library: 32tr, 32bc, 39br, 63tl; Jamstec 66cl; **© Japanese Meteorological Agency**/ Meteorological Office 12l; **Frank Lane Photo Agency**/M. Neqwman 11br; **National Oceanography centre, Southampton:** 53tr; **Nature Picture Library:** David Shale 70t Doc White 65b, Fabio Liverani 65tr, Ieff Foott 69cl, Peter Scoones 65cl, Thomas D. Mangelsen 69b; **naturepl.com:** Oceanwide / Gary Bell 33cra, David Shale 43br, Norbert Wu 11t, 44b; **Science Photo Library:** Dr. G. Feldman 26bl, Ron Church 53tl, Douglas Faulkner 66cr, Simon Fraser 62cl, NASA/Goddard Space Flight Centre 70br, Tom Van Sant, Geosphere Project/ Planetary, Visions 64cl, Patrick Landmann 54c, Natural History Museum, London 45tc, Nature Picture Library / Michael Pitts 61tr, Peter Scoones 38crb, Southampton Oceanography Centre / B. Murton 46cl, Stan Wayman 47cra; **Frank Spooner Pictures:** 54bl

All other images © Dorling Kindersley.
For further information see:
www.dkimages.com